Mindful Productivity: Cultivating Quality Work, Achieving balance and Sustainable Habits for Lasting Success"

Bonus Tips:10 Tips in building from scratch in productivity

By Robert H Clark

Mindful Productivity: Cultivating Quality Work, Achieving balance and Sustainable Habits for Lasting Success

Copyright

All rights reserved, no part of this publication may be reproduced, distributed or transmitted in any form or by any means, including photocopying, recording or other electronic or m echanical methods, without the prior written permission of the publisher, except in the case if Brier quotations embodied in critical reviews and certain other non commercial uses permitted by copyright law

Copyright @(Robert H Clark)(2024)

Disclaimer

Disclaimer: The information provided in this book, "Mindful productivity" is intended for general informational purposes only. It is not a substitute for professional medical advice, diagnosis, or treatment. Always seek the advice of your physician or qualified health provider with any questions you may have regarding a medical condition. The author and publisher do not endorse specific treatments or procedures mentioned in this guide, and they are not liable for any consequences resulting

Mindful Productivity: Cultivating Quality Work, Achieving balance and Sustainable Habits for Lasting Success

About the book

In "Mindful Productivity: Cultivating Quality Work, Achieving balance and Sustainable Habits for Lasting Success"",readers are invited to challenge the prevailing notion that productivity is solely about doing more in less time. Instead, the book introduces the concept of slow productivity—a philosophy that prioritizes quality over quantity, and emphasizes working at a natural pace to cultivate greater fulfillment and satisfaction.

Drawing on principles from mindfulness, personal development, and productivity literature, this book offers practical strategies and insights for integrating slow productivity into everyday life. From time blocking techniques and goal setting exercises to mindfulness practices and strategies for overcoming resistance, readers will discover a wealth of tools and resources to help them slow down, focus on what truly matters, and lead a more intentional and purposeful life.

Mindful Productivity: Cultivating Quality Work, Achieving balance and Sustainable Habits for Lasting Success

Through relatable anecdotes, actionable advice, and thought-provoking exercises, "finding the flow" provides readers with the inspiration and guidance they need to break free from the culture of busyness, reclaim control over their time and priorities, and cultivate a deeper sense of meaning and fulfillment in their work and lives.

Whether you're feeling overwhelmed by the pressures of modern life or simply seeking a more balanced and fulfilling approach to productivity, "Mindful Productivity: Cultivating Quality Work, Achieving balance and Sustainable Habits for Lasting Success" for Lasting Fulfillment"offers a roadmap for embracing a slower, more intentional way of living and working—one deliberate step at a time.

Mindful Productivity: Cultivating Quality Work, Achieving balance and Sustainable Habits for Lasting Success

About the author

Robert H. Clark is a prolific author, speaker, and thought leader in the fields of productivity, personal development, and mindfulness. With a passion for helping others live more intentional and fulfilling lives, Clark has dedicated his career to exploring innovative approaches to work, productivity, and well-being.

Born and raised in a small town in the Midwest, Clark developed an early fascination with the intersection of psychology, philosophy, and productivity. He pursued his academic studies at prestigious institutions, earning degrees in psychology and business administration, and later completing advanced training in mindfulness and coaching.

Throughout his career, Clark has held various roles in both corporate and nonprofit sectors, gaining valuable insights into the challenges and opportunities facing individuals and organizations in today's fast-paced world. Drawing on his diverse background and experiences, he has authored several bestselling books, including "Slow Productivity: Embracing a Fulfilling Approach to Work and Life," which has received widespread acclaim for its practical wisdom and actionable advice.

In addition to his writing, Clark is a sought-after speaker and consultant, delivering keynote presentations, workshops, and training programs to audiences around the world. He is known for his engaging and insightful speaking style, as well as his ability to connect with audiences on a personal level.

Clark's work is guided by a deep commitment to helping others unlock their full potential,

Mindful Productivity: Cultivating Quality Work, Achieving balance and Sustainable Habits for Lasting Success

cultivate resilience, and lead more purposeful and meaningful lives. Through his writing, speaking, and coaching, he continues to inspire and empower individuals to embrace slow productivity, prioritize what truly matters, and find fulfillment in both their work and their lives.

Mindful Productivity: Cultivating Quality Work, Achieving balance and Sustainable Habits for Lasting Success

Bonus Tips: 10 Strategies for Building Productivity from Scratch

Building productivity from scratch can be a daunting task, but with the right strategies and mindset, it's entirely achievable. In this bonus section, we'll explore ten practical tips to help you lay the foundation for a more productive and fulfilling life, whether you're starting from square one or looking to enhance your existing habits and routines.

1. Start with Why:

   - Before diving into productivity techniques and tools, take some time to reflect on your why. What motivates you to become more productive? What goals are you striving to achieve? Understanding your underlying motivations will give you clarity and purpose as you embark on your productivity journey.

2. Set Clear Goals:

   - Establish clear, specific goals that align with your values and aspirations. Break down larger goals into smaller, actionable steps, and create timelines and deadlines to keep yourself accountable. Having a clear direction will help you stay focused and motivated as you work towards your objectives.

3. Prioritize Tasks:

- Learn to distinguish between tasks that are important and urgent versus those that are merely distractions. Prioritize your tasks based on their significance and impact, and focus your time and energy on activities that align with your goals and priorities.

4. Develop a Routine:

- Establishing a daily routine can provide structure and consistency to your days, making it easier to stay on track and accomplish your tasks. Identify the key activities and habits you want to incorporate into your routine, and commit to sticking to it consistently.

5. Practice Time Blocking:

- Time blocking involves scheduling specific blocks of time for different tasks or activities throughout your day. By allocating dedicated time to focus on specific tasks, you can minimize distractions and improve your productivity and focus.

Mindful Productivity: Cultivating Quality Work, Achieving balance and Sustainable Habits for Lasting Success

6. Embrace Single-tasking:

   - Multitasking may seem efficient, but it often leads to decreased productivity and poorer quality of work. Instead, embrace the practice of single-tasking—focusing on one task at a time and giving it your full attention until completion.

7. Take Regular Breaks:

   - Avoid burnout and maintain your energy levels by taking regular breaks throughout your day. Schedule short breaks to rest and recharge, and use longer breaks for activities that help you relax and unwind.

8. Cultivate Mindfulness:

   - Mindfulness involves being fully present and engaged in the moment, without judgment. Incorporate mindfulness practices into your daily routine, such as meditation, deep breathing exercises, or mindful walking, to enhance your focus and reduce stress.

9. Stay Organized:

   - Keep your workspace and digital files organized to minimize distractions and streamline your workflow. Develop systems and processes for managing your tasks, emails, and documents effectively, and regularly declutter and review your systems to ensure they remain efficient.

10. Celebrate Progress:

   - Finally, celebrate your progress and accomplishments along the way. Acknowledge your efforts and achievements, no matter how small, and use them as motivation to continue striving towards your goals. Remember that building productivity is a journey, and every step forward is a cause for celebration.

Building productivity from scratch requires commitment, effort, and perseverance, but the rewards are well worth it. By implementing these ten strategies into your daily life, you can lay the foundation for a more productive, fulfilling, and purposeful existence. So, start today, take small steps towards your goals, and watch as your productivity and success soar.

Mindful Productivity: Cultivating Quality Work, Achieving balance and Sustainable Habits for Lasting Success

About the book.. 3
About the author... 6
Introduction... 15
Chapter 1... 20
    Rethinking Productivity in the Modern Age............. 20
Chapter 2:... 27
    The Pitfalls of Busyness: Understanding the Problem 27
Chapter 3... 38
    Lessons from History: Traditional Approaches to Productivity... 38
Chapter 4:... 46
    Principles of Slow Productivity................................ 46
Chapter 5:... 59
    Rethinking Workload Management......................... 59
Chapter 6:... 76
    Introducing Seasonal Variation:............................... 76
Chapter 7... 102
    Shifting Towards Long-Term Quality:.................... 102
Chapter 8... 127
Chapter 9... 146
    Overcoming Resistance: Navigating Challenges and Unlocking Success.. 146
Chapter 10... 153
    Embracing Slow Productivity: Cultivating Fulfillment and Success in a Fast-Paced World..................... 153
Conclusion:... 159

Mindful Productivity: Cultivating Quality Work, Achieving balance and Sustainable Habits for Lasting Success

Introduction

Title: Mindful Productivity: Cultivating Quality Work, Achieving balance and Sustainable Habits for Lasting Success"Are you sick and weary of constantly chasing after work and never feeling like you've accomplished anything? It's time for a productivity revolution in a society that exalts busyness and frequently experiences burnout. Let us now introduce you to "Finding Flow: Embracing the Ease of Slow Productivity for Lasting Fulfillment."This book is a manifesto for recovering your sanity and rediscovering the joy of meaningful work—it's not simply another time management manual. Come along with us as we set out to overcome the rush culture and adopt a calmer, more sustainable method of production that puts quality before quantity and enables you to succeed without compromising your wellbeing.

A path less taken but infinitely more gratifying is illuminated by the idea of slow productivity, which emerges as a beacon of hope in a society where busyness is celebrated and burnout is all

Mindful Productivity: Cultivating Quality Work, Achieving balance and Sustainable Habits for Lasting Success

too common due to the persistent pursuit of production. We set out on a voyage of inquiry and revelation in the pages that follow, delving deeply into the core of sluggish productivity and discovering its revolutionary potential to change our lives, our jobs, and our entire planet.

Let's take a moment to consider the current status of productivity in the modern day before delving into the specifics of slow productivity. The lines between work and play have become increasingly hazy in our constantly connected world, and performance expectations are unrelenting. We are locked in a never-ending loop of busyness, always wanting to be more, do more, and achieve more, but we never seem to be able to catch up.

This sense of urgency has only been made worse by the development of technology, which has left us constantly besieged with alerts, emails, and requests for our time. The pressure to always be accessible, responsive, and productive is thrown at us from all directions. Furthermore, we forfeit not only our well-being and sense of fulfillment but also our time and energy in an

Mindful Productivity: Cultivating Quality Work, Achieving balance and Sustainable Habits for Lasting Success

attempt to keep up with the unrelenting pace of modern life.

Still, what if there's an alternative? What if we adopted a slower, more deliberate approach to work and life, one that values sustainability over speed, quality over quantity, and mindfulness over multitasking, rather than giving in to the tyranny of production at all costs? What if we determined our value based on the relationships we create, the lives we touch, and the effect we make rather than the amount of work we accomplish or the number of hours we put in?

This is the promise of slow productivity, a promise that is both more pertinent and pressing now than it has ever been and is grounded in the knowledge of ancient times. We shall delve into the concepts of slow production in the pages that follow, taking our cues from the timeless insights of the most influential and inventive people in history. We shall discover the techniques of individuals who have perfected the craft of creating meaningful work with longevity, from the methodical routines of Maya

Mindful Productivity: Cultivating Quality Work, Achieving balance and Sustainable Habits for Lasting Success

Angelou to the thoughtful practices of Leonardo da Vinci.

However, slow productivity is a way of living rather than merely a philosophy or a set of guidelines. It's about taking back our time, our vitality, and our humanity in a world that frequently seems determined to take it all away. It's about redefining success according to our own standards and discovering fulfillment in meaningful work that uplifts others around us and feeds our souls, rather than in the never-ending chase of production for its own sake.

So come along on this voyage with me, dear reader. A calmer, more sustainable approach to productivity—a style of working and living that respects our humanity, fosters our creativity, and enriches our lives in ways we never imagined possible—should be adopted as we free ourselves from the chains of activity and overwhelm. Come explore with me how sluggish productivity may change the world and our work at the same time.

Mindful Productivity: Cultivating Quality Work, Achieving balance and Sustainable Habits for Lasting Success

Chapter 1

Rethinking Productivity in the Modern Age

The pursuit of productivity has intensified in today's fast-paced world. In our culture, being busy is highly valued, and being successful is frequently associated with being active and never stopping. We are inundated with messages asking us to work more, put in more hours, and aim for maximum efficiency in everything we do from the moment we wake up until the moment we go to bed. However, in our constant attempt to keep up with this fast-paced environment, we frequently find ourselves feeling overburdened, anxious, and worn out all the time.

This sense of urgency has only grown as a result of technology, which has blurred the boundaries between work and play and made it harder and harder to switch off and relax. We feel as though we are always on call and at the beck and call of our devices because we are inundated with emails, notifications, and requests for our time.

Mindful Productivity: Cultivating Quality Work, Achieving balance and Sustainable Habits for Lasting Success

However, in the middle of this mayhem, an increasing number of people are asking us to stop, slow down, and reevaluate how we approach productivity. They contend that we have been misled by the unrelenting quest of optimization and efficiency, sacrificing our mental health and well-being in the name of output.

Slow production is a movement that questions the idea that speed is always preferable. It promotes a more sustainable, well-balanced way of living and working that puts wellbeing above material possessions, presence before production, and quality above quantity.

Regaining our time, our energy, and our humanity in a world that frequently seems determined to take them away is the fundamental goal of slow productivity. It's about accepting the notion that productivity doesn't require perpetual busyness and that real achievement entails more than simply crossing tasks off a to-do list.

We'll examine the ideas behind delayed productivity on the pages that follow and see

Mindful Productivity: Cultivating Quality Work, Achieving balance and Sustainable Habits for Lasting Success

how they can improve our quality of life. We'll discover how to prioritize our work, set limits, and develop perspective and balance in both our personal and professional life.

We'll also look at the psychological effects of our fixation with output, including the growth in stress and anxiety as well as the global burnout pandemic that is rife in workplaces. And we'll find workable solutions to these problems so we can get back our time, energy, and sanity.

So come along with us as we set out to reevaluate productivity in the contemporary era. Together, let's push back against the status quo and adopt a more deliberate, calmer approach to life and work—one that celebrates our humanity, fosters our creativity, and enables us to survive in a society that frequently seems set on pushing us to the verge of burnout.

What does the term "modern age" actually mean?

Recognizing the Modern Era

The Renaissance and the Age of Discovery, which generally started in the late 15th century and continued to the present, are referred to as the "modern age" in history. It is distinguished by notable developments in science, technology, industry, and culture, as well as important shifts in social and political structures that have molded the modern world.

The expansion of industry and the advent of capitalism are two characteristics that characterize the modern era. During this time, new economic systems centered on free markets and private ownership came into being. Additionally, factories, technology, and mass production techniques were developed, revolutionizing the production and consumption of products. Along with previously unheard-of levels of economic growth and wealth, these adjustments brought forth fresh manifestations of exploitation, inequality, and social upheaval.

Significant changes in the political environment were also observed in the modern era, including the emergence of nation-states, the dissemination of democratic principles, and the collapse of conventional forms of authority like monarchy and feudalism. Modern political doctrines including nationalism, socialism, and liberalism emerged during this time and have since shaped contemporary political debate and environments.

Another characteristic of the modern era was the progress made in science and technology. Significant advances in physics, chemistry, biology, and medicine occurred during this time, which greatly enhanced our comprehension of the natural world and our capacity to influence it for our own gain. In addition, throughout this time period, revolutionary technologies like the internet, telephones, steam engines, and electricity were developed. These innovations completely changed the way people interact, work, and live.

The modern era was characterized by creativity, experimentation, and discovery in terms of culture. The arts, music, literature, philosophy, and modernism all flourished during this time, while new concepts and movements like modernism, romanticism, and enlightenment also gained popularity. During this period, there was a great deal of creative and intellectual ferment as intellectuals and artists tried to make sense of the world in novel and exciting ways while grappling with the enormous changes that were occurring all around them.

However, the modern era has also brought up new difficulties and crises in addition to these victories and accomplishments. Devastating wars like the World Wars occurred during this time, along with economic downturns, environmental damage, and social unrest. These difficulties still face us now, serving as a constant reminder that the contemporary era is marked by hardship and uncertainty in addition to development and progress.

In summary, the modern era is a complicated and diverse historical period that has had a significant and long-lasting influence on the world we live in today. This is a period of enormous developments and successes, but it is also one of enormous problems and uncertainty. Making sense of the world we live in and navigating its intricacies requires an understanding of the modern era.

Chapter 2:

The Pitfalls of Busyness: Understanding the Problem

What does the phrase "pitfalls of busyness" mean? The term "pitfalls of busyness" describes the drawbacks or difficulties that result from being overly occupied or focused on a number of jobs or activities. This phrase implies that while being busy may occasionally be interpreted as an indication of success or production, it may also have negative effects if improperly handled.

These are some of the dangers of being too busy:

1. Burnout: Being overly busy all the time without taking pauses or putting self-care first can cause mental and physical tiredness, which in turn can lead to burnout.

2. Decreased productivity: Multitasking, which can result from being extremely busy, can lower productivity and quality of work. It may also lead to the hurry or neglect of crucial duties.

3. Stressed relationships: Feeling neglected or alone might result from being too busy to spend time with friends, family, or coworkers.

4. Reduced creativity: Being overly busy might make it difficult to ponder or think creatively, which can hinder one's capacity for creativity and problem-solving.

5. Health problems: Over time, neglecting one's physical and mental well-being owing to busy schedules can result in malnutrition, inadequate sleep, and exercise avoidance.

6. Missed opportunities: People who are too task-focused may pass up chances for networking, new experiences, or personal or professional development.

7. Lack of work-life balance: Being busy can make it difficult to distinguish between work and personal time, which makes it difficult to give priority to hobbies, relaxation, or leisure time.

It's critical to establish boundaries, delegate when appropriate, prioritize work wisely, and carve out time for fulfilling and well-being-promoting activities in order to prevent the negative effects of being overly busy.

Mindful Productivity: Cultivating Quality Work, Achieving balance and Sustainable Habits for Lasting Success

The Dangers of Being Overly Busy: Recognizing the Issue

In the fast-paced world of today, being busy is now seen as a virtue. We wear our full calendars and bursting to-do lists as badges of achievement, associating the sheer amount of work we have on our plates with our own personal worth. However, there are a number of unspoken risks and hazards that lurk beneath the surface of this obsession with busyness, endangering our health, our relationships, and our general quality of life.

The toll that busyness takes on our mental and emotional well-being is among its most sneaky drawbacks. We frequently find ourselves overburdened, anxious, and continually tired in our effort to accomplish more, be more, and achieve more. Feelings of worry, exhaustion, and even melancholy can result from the continual pressure to meet the expectations of modern living, which can be overwhelming.

Because we forgo sleep, exercise, and self-care in the sake of productivity, being busy can also have a negative impact on our physical health. A hectic lifestyle can lead to chronic stress and exhaustion, which can impair our immune systems, raise our chance of developing chronic illnesses like diabetes and heart disease, and perhaps shorten our lives. We frequently overlook the very things that are crucial for our health and well-being in our unrelenting quest of productivity, which puts us at danger of major problems in the future.

But the most sneaky drawback of being busy might be the damage it does to our interpersonal connections and relationships. We frequently forfeit valuable time with our loved ones and overlook the connections and people that are most important to us in our effort to keep up with our hectic schedules and overwhelming to-do lists. It's possible that we're always concerned and distracted, making it difficult for us to interact fully with those around us or to be in the present. Because it can be difficult to establish meaningful connections in the middle of our hectic lives, this can result in feelings of loneliness, isolation, and alienation.

Mindful Productivity: Cultivating Quality Work, Achieving balance and Sustainable Habits for Lasting Success

Busyness can negatively affect not just our relationships and health but also our general quality of life. We could lose out on the little pleasures in life, like slow walks in the park, introspective periods, or casual chats with friends, in our persistent quest of productivity. We can discover that we're trapped in a never-ending cycle of labor and consumption, always pushing ourselves to be better but never feeling fully content or contented.

In summary, there are a variety of hazards associated with being overly busy that jeopardize our general wellbeing, relationships, and health. Finding a remedy requires first understanding the issue, and in order to recover our time, energy, and humanity, we obviously need to reconsider how we approach success and productivity. We can escape the never-ending cycle of busyness and rediscover the joy and fulfillment that come from leading a more balanced and meaningful life by adopting a slower, more deliberate way of living that puts quality over quantity, presence over productivity, and connection over consumption.

Mindful Productivity: Cultivating Quality Work, Achieving balance and Sustainable Habits for Lasting Success

The main issue: One significant issue that sticks out above the others in today's society is the widespread culture of activity. This problem is negatively affecting our well-being, productivity, and general quality of life. It has permeated all part of our lives, including our relationships and place of employment.

The fundamental idea behind busyness culture is that productivity and achievement are indicated by a continuous state of busyness. Our ability to manage multiple things at once and the length of our to-do lists determine our value, leading us to associate activity with productivity and significance. However, this way of thinking has a price.

The effects of busyness culture on our mental and emotional well-being are among its main issues. Feelings of anxiety, stress, and burnout can result from the continual pressure to keep up with our hectic schedules and piled-high to-do lists. We always find ourselves in a state of perpetual activity, racing from one thing to the next without ever stopping to rest and refuel.

Mindful Productivity: Cultivating Quality Work, Achieving balance and Sustainable Habits for Lasting Success

Our mental and emotional health can suffer greatly from this ongoing stress, which can result in anxiety, depression, and other major health problems.

However, the issue affects not only our own health but also our social connections and relationships. We frequently disregard the people and relationships that are most important to us in an effort to keep up with our hectic schedules and forfeit valuable time with our loved ones. We can discover that we are unable to completely interact with those around us or to be in the present moment because we are continuously concerned and distracted. Because it can be difficult to establish meaningful connections in the middle of our hectic lives, this can result in feelings of loneliness, isolation, and alienation.

The influence that busyness culture has on our general efficacy and productivity is another significant issue. Contrary to popular assumption, productivity is not always correlated with constant busyness. Actually, the contrary is frequently true: when we're always hurrying

Mindful Productivity: Cultivating Quality Work, Achieving balance and Sustainable Habits for Lasting Success

from one work to the next, we're more prone to err, miss crucial details, and end up wasting time and energy on unimportant chores. Busyness culture really affects our ability to complete meaningful work and accomplish our goals by placing a higher value on quantity than quality.

However, the effect that busyness culture has on our general quality of life may be the largest issue with it. Our health, our relationships, and our happiness are often the things we have to give up in our never-ending quest of success and productivity. We find ourselves trapped in a never-ending cycle of labor and consumerism, never feeling fully pleased or fulfilled despite our relentless pursuit of more. Even though we may have all the signs of success—status, wealth, and worldly belongings—in our hearts, we question whether this is all there is to life and feel empty and unfulfilled.

In conclusion, whether we are aware of it or not, the culture of activity is a serious issue that impacts all of us. It's time to acknowledge the negative effects that being overly busy is having on our lives and to take steps to recover our

Mindful Productivity: Cultivating Quality Work, Achieving balance and Sustainable Habits for Lasting Success

humanity, our time, and our vitality. We can escape the never-ending cycle of busyness and rediscover the joy and fulfillment that come from leading a more balanced and meaningful life by adopting a slower, more deliberate approach to living—one that puts quality over quantity, presence over productivity, and connection over consumption.

Mindful Productivity: Cultivating Quality Work, Achieving balance and Sustainable Habits for Lasting Success

Chapter 3

Lessons from History: Traditional Approaches to Productivity

In our quest to understand productivity and find ways to optimize our efficiency in the modern age, we often overlook the wealth of wisdom that can be found in the traditions and practices of our ancestors. Throughout history, individuals and cultures around the world have developed their own unique approaches to productivity, rooted in principles of balance, intentionality, and connection to the natural world. By exploring these traditional approaches, we can gain valuable insights into how to cultivate a more sustainable and fulfilling way of working and living.

One of the key lessons we can learn from history is the importance of rhythm and routine. Many traditional cultures structured their daily lives around a natural rhythm of work and rest, aligning their activities with the cycles of the sun, the moon, and the seasons. They understood

Mindful Productivity: Cultivating Quality Work, Achieving balance and Sustainable Habits for Lasting Success

the value of pacing oneself, alternating periods of focused activity with periods of rest and renewal. By honoring these natural rhythms and embracing a more cyclical approach to productivity, we can avoid burnout and maintain a more sustainable level of energy and motivation over the long term.

Another lesson we can learn from history is the importance of craftsmanship and attention to detail. In many traditional societies, work was seen not just as a means to an end, but as a form of self-expression and a source of pride. Artisans and craftsmen would devote themselves wholeheartedly to their craft, striving for excellence in every detail of their work. They understood that true productivity is not just about getting things done, but about doing them well and taking pride in the quality of our workmanship. By embracing a similar mindset of craftsmanship and attention to detail in our own work, we can elevate the quality of our output and find greater satisfaction and fulfillment in what we do.

Mindful Productivity: Cultivating Quality Work, Achieving balance and Sustainable Habits for Lasting Success

Furthermore, traditional cultures often placed a strong emphasis on community and collaboration. People would come together to work on shared tasks and projects, pooling their resources and skills to achieve common goals. They understood the value of working together towards a common purpose, supporting one another and sharing the burden of work. By fostering a sense of community and collaboration in our own lives and workplaces, we can tap into the collective wisdom and creativity of the group, achieving more together than we ever could alone.

Finally, traditional approaches to productivity often emphasized the importance of mindfulness and presence in our work. Many ancient traditions, such as Buddhism and Taoism, teach the value of being fully present and engaged in the present moment, bringing a sense of mindfulness and awareness to everything we do. By cultivating a practice of mindfulness in our own lives, we can become more focused, more creative, and more effective in our work, finding greater satisfaction and fulfillment in the process.

In conclusion, the lessons from history offer valuable insights into how we can cultivate a more sustainable and fulfilling approach to productivity in the modern age. By honoring the natural rhythms of life, embracing craftsmanship and attention to detail, fostering community and collaboration, and cultivating mindfulness and presence in our work, we can unlock our full potential and achieve greater success and fulfillment in our lives.

Traditional approaches to productivity encompass a variety of practices and philosophies that have been developed and refined over centuries by cultures around the world. These approaches are often rooted in principles of balance, intentionality, and connection to the natural world. Here are some examples of traditional approaches to productivity:

1. Rituals and Routines: Many traditional cultures structured their daily lives around rituals and routines that helped them align their

activities with the natural rhythms of the day and the seasons. These rituals often included practices such as morning meditation or prayer, setting intentions for the day ahead, and reflecting on one's accomplishments and challenges at the end of the day. By establishing regular routines and rituals, individuals were able to create a sense of order and purpose in their lives, fostering greater productivity and well-being.

2. Work-Life Balance: Traditional cultures placed a strong emphasis on achieving balance between work, family, and leisure activities. They recognized the importance of taking time for rest and relaxation, as well as for meaningful connections with loved ones and community members. By prioritizing work-life balance, individuals were able to avoid burnout and maintain a more sustainable level of energy and motivation over the long term.

3. Craftsmanship and Attention to Detail: In many traditional societies, work was seen not just as a means to an end, but as a form of self-expression and a source of pride. Artisans

Mindful Productivity: Cultivating Quality Work, Achieving balance and Sustainable Habits for Lasting Success

and craftsmen would devote themselves wholeheartedly to their craft, striving for excellence in every detail of their work. They understood that true productivity is not just about getting things done, but about doing them well and taking pride in the quality of one's workmanship.

4. Community and Collaboration: Traditional cultures often placed a strong emphasis on community and collaboration, with people coming together to work on shared tasks and projects. By pooling their resources and skills, individuals were able to achieve common goals more efficiently and effectively than they ever could alone. This sense of community and collaboration fostered a spirit of mutual support and camaraderie, enhancing productivity and well-being for all involved.

5. Mindfulness and Presence: Many ancient traditions, such as Buddhism and Taoism, teach the value of being fully present and engaged in the present moment. By cultivating a practice of mindfulness and presence in their work and daily activities, individuals were able to increase their

focus, creativity, and effectiveness. They found greater satisfaction and fulfillment in their work, as well as a deeper sense of connection to themselves and the world around them.

Overall, traditional approaches to productivity emphasize the importance of balance, intentionality, and connection in our lives and work. By incorporating these principles into our own daily routines and practices, we can cultivate a more sustainable and fulfilling approach to productivity in the modern age.

Mindful Productivity: Cultivating Quality Work, Achieving balance and Sustainable Habits for Lasting Success

Chapter 4:

Principles of Slow Productivity

This chapter delves into the fundamental concepts and methods of slow productivity, examining the transformative methodology that guides this approach to work and life. We unearth the fundamental ideas that can help us recover our time, our energy, and our humanity in a world that frequently seems focused on robbing us of them by drawing on the knowledge of ages past as well as the insights of modern philosophers.

1. Quality above Quantity: The idea that quality should come first is the foundation of slow productivity. We place more emphasis on the caliber of our work and its influence on the world around us than on the quantity of things we finish or the amount of hours we work. By aiming for excellence in all we do, we may make contributions that are significant, long-lasting, and resilient.

Mindful Productivity: Cultivating Quality Work, Achieving balance and Sustainable Habits for Lasting Success

2. Intentionality and Purpose: Slow productivity pushes us to be purposeful and intentional in our work, ensuring that our activities are in line with our beliefs and objectives. Rather than blindly pursuing the next big thing or the newest productivity trend, we stop to consider what really matters to us and the reasons behind our actions. This feeling of purpose provides us with direction and clarity, enabling us to make meaningful and satisfying decisions and take action.

3. Mindfulness and Presence: Developing mindfulness and presence in our daily activities and work is a crucial component of slow productivity. By focusing our awareness and attention on the here and now, we can become more productive, focused, and creative. Our ability to respond more deftly and sensitively to opportunities and difficulties comes from our increased awareness of our own thoughts and feelings as well as the wants and wishes of people around us.

4. Boundaries and Balance: Slow productivity highlights how crucial it is to establish priorities

and balance in our life so that we can take care of our own needs and well-being. We understand the need of taking pauses, establishing boundaries, and saying no to activities that don't fit with our beliefs and objectives rather than always trying to do more and be more. We can prevent burnout and keep a longer-lasting level of energy and motivation by making time for relaxation and renewal.

5. Connection and Community: Lastly, delayed productivity pushes us to build ties and connections with people, realizing the need of cooperation and support in accomplishing our objectives. We see others as allies and collaborators on the path to significant accomplishment rather than as rivals or barriers to our success. We have the power to multiply our influence and bring about constructive change in the world by establishing robust support and collaboration networks.

To sum up, the slow productivity principles provide a strong foundation for rethinking how we approach both work and life. We may design more balanced, purposeful, and happy lives by emphasizing quality over quantity, developing intentionality and purpose, being conscious and present, establishing limits and priorities, and encouraging community and connection. Slow productivity is a style of living and working that respects our humanity, fosters our creativity, and enables us to flourish in a world that frequently seems intent on pushing us to the verge of fatigue. It is more than just a philosophy or a collection of techniques.

Please write the productivity principle for me. Reduce the number of things you do.

The Idea of Minimizing Activities

The idea of doing fewer things stands in stark contrast to a society that values busyness and associates productivity with the amount of work we can complete. It refutes the widely held belief that our level of success is determined by how much we can fit into our calendars and cross off our to-do lists. Rather, it encourages us to decelerate, streamline our lives, and concentrate on the things that really count.

Doing fewer things is fundamentally about making decisions and setting priorities. It's about

Mindful Productivity: Cultivating Quality Work, Achieving balance and Sustainable Habits for Lasting Success

realizing that we have limited resources—time and energy—and that we need to use them wisely. We concentrate on the few things that really matter—those pursuits that are consistent with our priorities, values, and aspirations—rather than exhausting ourselves attempting to do everything.

We make room for depth and excellence in our work and lives when we do fewer things. We may approach each activity or project with more care, inventiveness, and thoughtfulness because we can commit more time and attention to it. We may enjoy the process, immerse ourselves completely in the task at hand, and produce work of higher quality and greater impact rather than racing through it in a mad haste to get it all done. Regaining control over our time and sanity in a society that frequently seems to be trying to take them away is another benefit of doing less. We may make time for relaxation, renewal, and deep connections with people and ourselves rather than letting the never-ending pressures of modern life wear us out. We have the ability to take it easy, enjoy the here and now, and give thanks to the small things in life that make us happy and fulfilled.

Perhaps most crucial, though, is that the idea of doing fewer things serves as a reminder that productivity is a tool rather than an end in and of itself. It's about living with intention and purpose, building rich, meaningful, and rewarding lives, and it goes beyond simply crossing things off a to-do list or working as efficiently as possible. We can concentrate on what really important and match our actions with our innermost goals and ideals when we do fewer things.

In summary, the idea of doing fewer things is a potent remedy for the constant bustle and overwhelm that frequently define modern life. We can recover our time, our energy, and our humanity by putting quality over quantity and concentrating on the few things that truly matter. We can also build more balanced, purposeful, and happy lives by doing this.

The Natural Pace of Work Principle

Mindful Productivity: Cultivating Quality Work, Achieving balance and Sustainable Habits for Lasting Success

Working at your own pace is a welcome option in a world where things happen at a rapid pace. It questions the widely held belief that speed is always better and invites us to recognize the ebb and flow of our creative and energetic energies by tuning into our own rhythms and cycles. We can realize our greatest potential and reach higher degrees of output, fulfillment, and wellbeing by working at a pace that feels genuine and sustainable.

Fundamentally, working at a natural pace involves coordinating our activities with life's inherent cycles. It's about realizing that we all have periods of time when we are inherently more focused and energized and periods when we require rest and renewal. We pay attention to our internal cues and modify our workflow in response, rather than pushing ourselves to work at a relentlessly fast pace.

Resisting the need to be active and productive all the time is another aspect of working at a natural pace. It's about realizing that leisure and downtime are necessary for our health and that we should make time in our life for

Mindful Productivity: Cultivating Quality Work, Achieving balance and Sustainable Habits for Lasting Success

introspection, rest, and relaxation. We can avoid burnout and preserve a longer-lasting, more sustainable level of energy and enthusiasm by allowing ourselves to take breaks and rejuvenate. Most crucial, though, is that working at our own pace lets us use our inherent creativity and intuition. Rushing from one work to the next prevents us from giving ourselves the time and space we need to reflect deeply, consider novel concepts, or try out various strategies. We can foster an environment that is conducive to creativity and innovation by taking our time and working at a more relaxed pace.

To sum up, the idea of working at a natural pace provides a strong foundation for rethinking how we approach both work and life. We may realize our full potential and increase our levels of productivity, happiness, and well-being by connecting with our natural rhythms and cycles, respecting the need for rest and relaxation, and making room for creativity and intuition to grow. Working at a natural pace allows us to live more fully, truly, and in harmony with our actual selves, rather than just getting more done.

Mindful Productivity: Cultivating Quality Work, Achieving balance and Sustainable Habits for Lasting Success

The Obsess over Quality Principle

The idea of obsessing over quality serves as a potent reminder of the value of workmanship, attention to detail, and the pursuit of perfection in all that we do in a society where speed and quantity frequently take precedence over depth and excellence. It pushes us to pursue the greatest levels of quality in both our professional and personal lives, resisting the urge to skimp or settle for mediocrity.

Fundamentally, being obsessed with quality is about having an unwavering dedication to greatness. Whether or not anyone is watching or keeping score, it's about having pride in our work and holding ourselves to the greatest standards of honesty and quality. It's about realizing that the quality of our efforts and the influence they have on the world around us bring us true contentment and satisfaction rather than the amount of things we achieve.

To be willing to put in the time and effort required to produce our finest work is another aspect of having a quality obsession. It involves investing the necessary time to fully develop our talents, become experts in our fields, and sharpen our skills. It involves adopting a philosophy of lifelong learning and continual growth in order to consistently raise the bar and beyond our own expectations.

The fact that we are extremely concerned about the results of our work and how it affects other people is possibly the most significant aspect of our obsession with excellence. Realizing that the people in our immediate vicinity can be inspired, uplifted, and positively impacted by our job is crucial. Whether we're producing art, finding a solution to a challenging problem, or just doing our hardest on a daily basis, we have the chance to leave a remarkable legacy that will go on long after we're gone.

Finally, the quality obsession concept provides a strong foundation for rethinking how we approach our work and lives. Rich, meaningful, and deeply rewarding lives can be created by embracing a tireless commitment to craftsmanship and integrity, and by putting perfection over expediency. Quality obsession is about more than just creating better work; it's

Mindful Productivity: Cultivating Quality Work, Achieving balance and Sustainable Habits for Lasting Success

about living a purposeful, intentional life and using the power of our own excellence to positively influence the world around us.

Chapter 5:

Rethinking Workload Management.

This chapter delves into the crucial subject of workload management, examining how we might change the way we approach work to attain higher levels of effectiveness, well-being, and balance. It is more crucial than ever to create techniques for managing our workload in a sustainable and rewarding way because job demands seem to be rising everywhere.

The significance of establishing boundaries and priorities is one of the important lessons we'll discuss in this chapter. We'll learn how to prioritize our time and energy by identifying the chores and projects that are genuinely vital, as opposed to trying to do everything at once. We may prevent overstretching ourselves and make sure we have time for the things that really matter by establishing boundaries around our job and declining assignments that don't fit with our priorities.

Mindful Productivity: Cultivating Quality Work, Achieving balance and Sustainable Habits for Lasting Success

Pacing oneself and avoiding the overwork trap is another crucial component in reevaluating task management. It might be easy to push ourselves to the point of exhaustion in the name of achieving our goals in a society that values busyness and associates long hours with productivity. However, this strategy is not only unworkable but also ineffective. We can avoid burnout and retain a longer-lasting, more sustainable level of energy and motivation by appreciating the importance of relaxation and renewal and making time in our life for leisure and quiet.

We'll also look at how technology has influenced our methods for managing our workloads and how we may get the most of it without being overwhelmed. Technology has completely changed the way we work, from social media and email to project management software and productivity apps. However, it has also brought out a number of new difficulties and diversions that can make it more difficult to efficiently manage our workload. We can use technology to improve our productivity and effectiveness without compromising our wellbeing if we embrace techniques for handling digital overload and use it thoughtfully.

Lastly, we'll look at how crucial delegation and teamwork are to efficient workload management. We'll learn how to take advantage of the skills and talents of others rather than attempting to accomplish everything ourselves in order to accomplish our objectives more quickly and successfully. Strengthening our support systems and working together on common goals will enable us to make a bigger difference and succeed more than we ever could working alone.

To sum up, reevaluating workload management is crucial to negotiating the intricacies of the contemporary workplace and obtaining increased effectiveness, balance, and wellbeing. We may create workload management strategies that enable us to flourish in both our work and personal life by establishing boundaries and priorities, pacing ourselves, using technology thoughtfully, and working with others.

The Techniques of Prioritization

Mindful Productivity: Cultivating Quality Work, Achieving balance and Sustainable Habits for Lasting Success

Prioritization Techniques: Using Your Time and Energy to the Fullest

Learning the skill of prioritization is crucial for success and wellbeing in the fast-paced world we live in, where demands on our time and attention are always rising. By concentrating our time and efforts on the projects and activities that will have the biggest effects, prioritization techniques help us reach our objectives more quickly and successfully. We'll look at a few important prioritization techniques in this section to help you maximize your time and productivity.

1. Eisenhower Matrix: Also referred to as the Urgent-Important Matrix, the Eisenhower Matrix is a useful tool for setting priorities for tasks according to their importance and urgency. There are four categories for tasks: neither urgent nor important, urgent but not important, important but not urgent, and urgent and not important. You may make sure that your time and energy are being used most effectively by concentrating on the first quadrant of work—those that are both urgent and

important—and assigning or removing jobs from the other quadrants.

2. ABCDE approach: This approach of prioritization also assists you in identifying and ranking projects according to their importance and due dates. Based on their relative importance, tasks are graded with a letter (A, B, C, D, or E), where A tasks are the most significant and E tasks are the least important. Within each category, projects are then further ranked according to their deadlines; those with closer deadlines are given priority over those with longer lead times. You may make sure that you're tackling the most crucial chores first and moving steadily closer to your goals by concentrating on finishing your A tasks first and working your way down the list.

3. The 80/20 Rule: Also referred to as the Pareto Principle, this rule indicates that about 80% of the outcomes are the result of 20% of the efforts. When it comes to prioritization, this entails determining which projects and activities will have the most effects on your objectives and concentrating your time and efforts on them.

Mindful Productivity: Cultivating Quality Work, Achieving balance and Sustainable Habits for Lasting Success

You may increase your productivity and effectiveness by figuring out which 20% of the tasks will provide 80% of the results and ranking them accordingly.

4. Time Blocking: This strategy entails allocating particular time blocks for various assignments or pursuits. You may make sure that you're working on your most critical duties without becoming sidetracked or overwhelmed by blocking aside time for concentrated work, meetings, email, and other activities. Making the most of your time and energy is possible when you implement time blocking to help you establish discipline and organization in your day.

5. The Four Ds: The Four Ds are a straightforward framework for choosing how to handle each task that comes your way. They are Do, Defer, Delegate, and Delete. When a task is essential and significant, you complete it right away. You put things off till later if it's not urgent but nonetheless important. If it's not critical yet urgent, assign it to someone else. You cross anything off your to-do list completely if it's not urgent or important. You can make sure

that you're devoting your time and effort to the projects that will have the biggest impact by using the Four Ds to every work.

In conclusion, developing efficient prioritization techniques is crucial for time and energy management in the fast-paced world of today. Utilizing techniques such as the Eisenhower Matrix, the ABCDE method, the 80/20 rule, time blocking, and the Four Ds, you may prioritize your work, manage your resources effectively, and move closer to your objectives. By implementing efficient prioritization techniques, you can attain improved equilibrium, productivity, and welfare in both your professional and personal life.

Having reasonable expectations is essential for both success and wellbeing.

Setting oneself up for failure is a common temptation we encounter in our quest of success and productivity. We want to be able to accomplish everything swiftly and with ease. We want to have everything and do everything. But we put ourselves in a position to experience disappointment, annoyance, and fatigue when our expectations are not in line with reality. Maintaining our well-being, controlling our stress levels, and reaching our goals in a sustainable manner all depend on having reasonable expectations.

1. Recognize Your Limits: Knowing your personal limitations, in terms of both time and energy, is the first step toward establishing reasonable expectations. When it comes to how much you can actually get done in a day or a week, be honest with yourself and don't try to do more than you can manage. Acknowledge your humanity and accept that you should pace yourself and take pauses when required.

2. Pay Attention to What's Achievable: Rather than attempting to complete everything at once, pay attention to what is feasible in light of your existing resources and situation. Establish reasonable, quantifiable goals and divide them into smaller, more doable activities. You may move closer to your goals without feeling overwhelmed if you concentrate on what you can control and what is doable in the near future.

Mindful Productivity: Cultivating Quality Work, Achieving balance and Sustainable Habits for Lasting Success

3. Be Adaptable and Flexible: Things don't always go as planned in life since life is unpredictable. Be adaptable to changing circumstances rather than tightly holding onto your assumptions. Along the journey, there may be new opportunities and options, so be open to exploring them and ready to modify your priorities and goals as necessary. It is possible to handle life's ups and downs with grace and resilience if you adopt an attitude of adaptation and flexibility.

4. Use Your Time Sensibly: To achieve your goals and create reasonable expectations, time management is essential. Make deliberate decisions about how to spend your time and energy, and rank things according to their urgency and significance. Make time in your schedule for meetings, concentrated work, and self-care, and pay attention to how you use your time throughout the day. You may make sure that you're moving toward your goals without compromising your wellbeing by practicing effective time management.

Mindful Productivity: Cultivating Quality Work, Achieving balance and Sustainable Habits for Lasting Success

5. Honor advancement rather than perfection:Lastly, never forget to acknowledge and celebrate any accomplishment, no matter how tiny. Celebrate the little successes along the way, such as the chores you finish, the milestones you accomplish, and the lessons you learn, rather than concentrating on perfection or the final product. You can maintain your motivation and inspiration to keep going forward even when things get difficult by recognizing and appreciating your accomplishments.

In conclusion, in today's fast-paced environment, having reasonable expectations is crucial for both success and wellbeing. You can position yourself for success and accomplish your goals in a lasting and satisfying fashion by being aware of your limitations, concentrating on what is attainable, exercising flexibility and adaptability, making good use of your time, and acknowledging your accomplishments. Setting reasonable expectations can help you face life's obstacles head-on and bounce back from setbacks, believing that little by little, you can accomplish great things.

Accepting Limitations to Unleash Innovation and Creativity

A common perception of constraints is that they are impediments that must be surmounted, that prevent us from realizing our greatest potential. However, what if we adopted the opposite viewpoint and viewed limitations as chances for creativity and innovation? Embracing restrictions means reinterpreting them as growth-promoting forces that enable us to think creatively beyond the box, investigate novel avenues, and realize our full creative potential.

1. Clarity and Focus: We are compelled by constraints to prioritize things and focus our attention. We're forced to focus on what's really important and let rid of diversions and non-essentials when we're faced with time, resource, or scope constraints. We can direct our creativity and energy toward the most significant answers when we have a clear focus, which produces more creative and successful results.

2. Creativity Through Limitation: Despite common assumption, creativity flourishes in the

face of limitations. When faced with constraints, we have to use our imaginations to come up with novel ways to get around them. Limitations inspire us to think creatively, consider things from fresh angles, and stretch the bounds of what's feasible. In fact, working under strict limitations has driven inventors and creators to come up with creative solutions to issues that seemed insurmountable, leading to some of the most revolutionary inventions in history.

3. Resourcefulness and Ingenuity: Learning to live with limitations encourages us to be resourceful and inventive, making the most of what we have. When time or resources are scarce, we must come up with innovative solutions to make the most of them and accomplish our objectives. In addition to assisting us in overcoming current obstacles, this inventive and resourceful mindset also strengthens our resilience and flexibility, positioning us to prosper in the face of uncertainty and change.

4. creativity and Iteration: By encouraging a culture of experimentation and iteration,

constraints promote creativity. When faced with constraints, we tend to be more open to trying new things, taking calculated chances, and picking up lessons from mistakes. Adopting an experimental and iteration mindset allows us to quickly hone concepts, improve methods, and find fresh perspectives that result in game-changing breakthroughs.

5. Concentrate on What Matters Most: Maybe most significantly, accepting limitations enables us to concentrate on what really counts most. We can focus on our main values, priorities, and objectives when we are relieved of the weight of limitless options. We can make more deliberate judgments, match our activities to our beliefs, and have a significant impact on the world when we have a clear sense of our purpose.

To sum up, accepting restrictions means using them to fuel growth, innovation, and creativity rather than accepting them as unavoidable. We may reach our full potential and experience more success and fulfillment in both our personal and professional lives by reinterpreting limitations as chances for concentration, creativity, resourcefulness, and invention. Limitations aren't what make people creative or innovative; rather, constraints encourage us to think outside the box, consider novel options, and, in the end, persevere in the face of difficulty.

Mindful Productivity: Cultivating Quality Work, Achieving balance and Sustainable Habits for Lasting Success

Chapter 6:

Introducing Seasonal Variation:

Harnessing the Power of Cycles for Productivity and Well-being

Seasonal variation is a concept that emphasizes the importance of aligning our activities and rhythms with the natural cycles of the seasons. Just as nature goes through cycles of growth, rest, and renewal throughout the year, so too can we benefit from incorporating seasonal variation into our lives and work. By tuning into the changing seasons and adapting our habits and routines accordingly, we can optimize our productivity, creativity, and overall well-being.

1. Honoring Nature's Rhythms: Seasonal variation encourages us to honor the rhythms of nature and recognize the unique qualities and energy of each season. Just as spring is a time of growth and renewal, summer a time of abundance and activity, autumn a time of harvest and reflection, and winter a time of rest and introspection, so too can we align our activities

and priorities with the energy of each season. By embracing the natural ebb and flow of the seasons, we can harness their power to fuel our productivity and creativity throughout the year.

2. Adapting to Change: One of the key benefits of incorporating seasonal variation into our lives is its ability to help us adapt to change. Just as the seasons change and evolve over time, so too do our own needs, priorities, and goals. By embracing seasonal variation, we can create space for flexibility and adaptation, allowing us to adjust our habits and routines in response to changing circumstances and priorities. This adaptability enables us to stay nimble and resilient in the face of uncertainty and change, ensuring that we're able to thrive in any season.

3. Optimizing Productivity: Seasonal variation can also help us optimize our productivity by aligning our activities with the natural energy and rhythms of the seasons. For example, we might use the long, sunny days of summer to tackle outdoor projects and creative pursuits, while reserving the shorter, darker days of winter for introspection, planning, and rest. By tailoring

our activities to the energy of each season, we can work more efficiently and effectively, making the most of our time and resources.

4. Cultivating Well-being: In addition to enhancing productivity, seasonal variation can also promote overall well-being by fostering a deeper connection to nature and the world around us. Spending time outdoors, engaging in seasonal activities like gardening or hiking, and savoring seasonal foods can all contribute to a sense of vitality and fulfillment. By embracing the beauty and abundance of each season, we can nourish our bodies, minds, and spirits, and cultivate a greater sense of balance and harmony in our lives.

5. Creating Rituals and Traditions: Finally, incorporating seasonal variation into our lives can provide opportunities to create rituals and traditions that bring meaning and joy to our daily lives. Whether it's celebrating the changing of the seasons with family and friends, observing seasonal holidays and festivals, or simply taking time to appreciate the beauty of nature, these rituals can help us feel connected to something

Mindful Productivity: Cultivating Quality Work, Achieving balance and Sustainable Habits for Lasting Success

larger than ourselves and infuse our lives with a sense of purpose and wonder.

In conclusion, introducing seasonal variation into our lives and work offers a powerful way to harness the power of cycles for productivity, creativity, and well-being. By aligning our activities with the natural rhythms of the seasons, adapting to change, optimizing our productivity, cultivating well-being, and creating rituals and traditions, we can create lives that are more balanced, fulfilling, and connected to the world around us. Embracing seasonal variation is not just about following a set of rules or routines—it's about living in harmony with nature and embracing the beauty and abundance of each season, one day at a time.

In today's fast-paced world, where the demands of work and life seem to never cease, it's easy to feel overwhelmed and disconnected from the natural world around us. We live in a society that values constant productivity and busyness, often at the expense of our own well-being and the health of the planet. But what if there was another way? What if we could harness the

Mindful Productivity: Cultivating Quality Work, Achieving balance and Sustainable Habits for Lasting Success

power of nature's rhythms to enhance our productivity, creativity, and overall well-being? This is where the concept of embracing seasonal variation comes in.

Embracing seasonal variation is about recognizing and honoring the natural cycles of the seasons and aligning our activities and rhythms with them. Just as nature goes through cycles of growth, rest, and renewal throughout the year, so too can we benefit from incorporating seasonal variation into our lives and work. By tuning into the changing seasons and adapting our habits and routines accordingly, we can optimize our productivity, creativity, and overall well-being.

In this comprehensive guide, we'll explore the concept of seasonal variation in depth, examining its benefits, practical strategies for implementation, and tips for incorporating it into our daily lives. From understanding the unique qualities and energy of each season to adapting our work habits and routines to align with them, we'll delve into the ways in which embracing

Mindful Productivity: Cultivating Quality Work, Achieving balance and Sustainable Habits for Lasting Success

seasonal variation can transform the way we live, work, and thrive in the world.

Understanding the Seasons:

Before we can effectively embrace seasonal variation, it's important to understand the unique qualities and energy of each season. Each season has its own distinct characteristics, rhythms, and opportunities for growth and renewal. By gaining a deeper understanding of these qualities, we can better align our activities and priorities with the energy of each season, maximizing our productivity, creativity, and overall well-being.

Spring:

Spring is a time of growth, renewal, and new beginnings. As the days grow longer and the temperatures begin to warm, nature bursts forth in a riot of color and activity. It's a time of planting seeds, both literal and metaphorical, and laying the groundwork for future growth and expansion. In our own lives, spring is a time to set new goals, embark on new projects, and cultivate a sense of optimism and possibility.

Key Qualities of Spring:

Mindful Productivity: Cultivating Quality Work, Achieving balance and Sustainable Habits for Lasting Success

- Growth and Renewal: Spring is a time of new growth and renewal, both in nature and in our own lives. It's a time to shed the old and embrace the new, to plant seeds of intention and watch them bloom.
- Creativity and Inspiration: With the arrival of spring comes a sense of creativity and inspiration. As nature awakens from its winter slumber, so too do our own creative energies, leading to new ideas, projects, and possibilities.
- Action and Movement: Spring is a time of action and movement, as we shake off the lethargy of winter and begin to take proactive steps towards our goals. It's a time to harness the energy of the season and channel it into productive action.

Practical Tips for Embracing Spring:

1. Set new goals and intentions for the season ahead. Take some time to reflect on what you want to accomplish and set clear, actionable goals to help you get there.
2. Get outside and connect with nature. Take advantage of the longer days and warmer temperatures to spend time outdoors, soaking up

the energy of the season and rejuvenating your body and mind.

3. Cultivate a sense of optimism and possibility. Embrace the spirit of renewal and possibility that spring brings, and approach your work and life with a sense of enthusiasm and optimism.

Summer:

Summer is a time of abundance, vitality, and activity. As the days reach their longest and the sun shines bright in the sky, nature is in full bloom, teeming with life and energy. It's a time of harvest and celebration, of enjoying the fruits of our labor and basking in the warmth of the sun. In our own lives, summer is a time to capitalize on the energy of the season, to take action towards our goals, and to savor the joys of life.

Key Qualities of Summer:

- Abundance and Vitality: Summer is a time of abundance and vitality, as nature bursts forth in a riot of color and activity. It's a time to celebrate the richness and beauty of the world around us, and to revel in the joys of life.

Mindful Productivity: Cultivating Quality Work, Achieving balance and Sustainable Habits for Lasting Success

- Action and Momentum: With the long, sunny days of summer come a sense of action and momentum. It's a time to harness the energy of the season and take bold steps towards our goals, seizing opportunities and making the most of our resources.

- Joy and Celebration: Summer is a time of joy and celebration, as we gather with loved ones, enjoy outdoor activities, and savor the simple pleasures of life. It's a time to embrace the spirit of fun and adventure, and to make the most of every moment.

Practical Tips for Embracing Summer:

1. Take action towards your goals. Use the energy of the season to make progress on your projects and pursue your passions with enthusiasm and determination.

2. Spend time outdoors and enjoy the beauty of nature. Whether it's hiking in the mountains, lounging on the beach, or picnicking in the park, make time to connect with the natural world and soak up the energy of the season.

3. Cultivate a sense of gratitude and abundance. Take time each day to count your blessings and

appreciate the abundance of blessings in your life. Embrace the spirit of joy and reselience

Recognizing Cycles of Productivity: Understanding Patterns to Enhance Performance and Well-being

In today's fast-paced world, productivity has become synonymous with constant activity and relentless hustle. We're bombarded with messages urging us to do more, achieve more, and strive for peak performance at all times. But what if there was another way? What if we could unlock the secret to sustainable productivity by recognizing and honoring the natural cycles of productivity that govern our lives? This is where the concept of recognizing cycles of productivity comes in.

Recognizing cycles of productivity is about understanding the natural ebbs and flows of our energy, focus, and motivation, and aligning our activities and priorities accordingly. Just as nature goes through cycles of growth, rest, and renewal, so too do we experience cycles of productivity, creativity, and well-being. By gaining a deeper understanding of these cycles and learning to work with them rather than against them, we can optimize our performance, enhance our well-being, and achieve greater success in all areas of our lives.

In this comprehensive guide, we'll explore the concept of recognizing cycles of productivity in depth, examining its benefits, practical strategies for implementation, and tips for incorporating it into our daily lives. From understanding the science behind our natural rhythms to identifying our own patterns of productivity, we'll delve into the ways in which recognizing cycles of productivity can transform the way we work, live, and thrive in the world.

Understanding the Science of Productivity Cycles:

Before we can effectively recognize cycles of productivity in our own lives, it's important to understand the science behind our natural rhythms and cycles. Our bodies and brains operate according to a variety of biological rhythms, including the circadian rhythm, the ultradian rhythm, and the infradian rhythm. By gaining a deeper understanding of these rhythms and how they impact our energy, focus, and productivity, we can better align our activities and priorities with our natural cycles of productivity.

1. Circadian Rhythm: The circadian rhythm is perhaps the most well-known biological rhythm, governing our sleep-wake cycle and influencing our energy levels and cognitive function throughout the day. Our circadian rhythm is regulated by an internal biological clock located in the suprachiasmatic nucleus of the brain, which responds to cues such as light and temperature to synchronize our internal rhythms with the external environment. By understanding our own circadian rhythm and how it influences our energy levels and cognitive function, we can optimize our daily schedule and maximize our productivity.

2. Ultradian Rhythm: In addition to the circadian rhythm, we also experience shorter cycles of productivity known as ultradian rhythms. Ultradian rhythms are characterized by recurring periods of high energy and focus followed by periods of rest and recovery. These cycles

typically last between 90 and 120 minutes and play a crucial role in regulating our energy levels and cognitive function throughout the day. By recognizing our own ultradian rhythms and structuring our work accordingly, we can optimize our productivity and avoid burnout.

3. Infradian Rhythm: Finally, we also experience longer cycles of productivity known as infradian rhythms. Infradian rhythms are characterized by recurring patterns of energy, mood, and behavior that occur over longer periods of time, such as days, weeks, or months. Examples of infradian rhythms include the menstrual cycle in women and the seasonal changes in mood and behavior that occur in response to changes in daylight and temperature. By recognizing our own infradian rhythms and how they influence our productivity and well-being, we can adjust our activities and priorities to align with these natural cycles.

Practical Strategies for Recognizing Cycles of Productivity:

Now that we have a better understanding of the science behind our natural rhythms and cycles, let's explore some practical strategies for recognizing cycles of productivity in our own lives:

1. Track Your Energy Levels:One of the most effective ways to recognize your own cycles of productivity is to track your energy levels throughout the day. Keep a journal or use a productivity app to record how you're feeling at different times of the day, noting any patterns or trends that emerge. Pay attention to when you feel most energized and focused, as well as when you experience dips in energy or motivation. By identifying your own natural rhythms, you can schedule your most important tasks and activities during times of peak productivity and plan for rest and recovery during periods of lower energy.

2. Experiment with Different Schedules:Experiment with different schedules and routines to see what works best for you. Some people may find that they're most productive in the morning, while others may be night owls who do their best work in the evening. Pay attention to when you feel most alert and focused, and structure your day

accordingly. You may also find that breaking your day into shorter blocks of focused work followed by brief breaks can help you maintain high levels of productivity throughout the day.

3. Listen to Your Body: Pay attention to your body's signals and cues, and honor its need for rest and recovery. If you're feeling tired or overwhelmed, take a short break to recharge your batteries and refocus your energy. Resist the urge to push through fatigue or work long hours without taking breaks, as this can lead to burnout

Adaptability in Action: Adjusting Workflows Accordingly for Optimal Productivity

In today's dynamic and fast-paced work environment, adaptability is a key factor in maintaining productivity and achieving success. As circumstances change, workflows that were once effective may become outdated or inefficient. Recognizing the need to adjust workflows accordingly is essential for staying competitive and maximizing productivity. In this comprehensive guide, we will explore the importance of adaptability in workflow management and provide practical strategies for adjusting workflows to ensure optimal productivity.

Understanding the Need for Adaptability:

The modern workplace is characterized by constant change, whether it's shifting priorities, evolving technologies, or unexpected disruptions. In such a dynamic environment, rigid workflows can quickly become obsolete, hindering rather than facilitating productivity. Recognizing the need for adaptability is the first step in ensuring that workflows remain effective and efficient.

1. Responding to Changing Priorities: One of the most common reasons for adjusting workflows is changes in priorities. As business objectives evolve or new opportunities arise, workflows must be flexible enough to accommodate these shifts. For example, a sudden change in market conditions may require a company to pivot its product development strategy, necessitating adjustments to workflow processes to ensure that resources are allocated appropriately and deadlines are met.

2. Embracing Technological Advancements: The rapid pace of technological advancement also necessitates regular adjustments to workflows. New tools and software solutions are constantly being developed to streamline processes and enhance efficiency. By embracing these advancements and integrating them into existing workflows, organizations can stay ahead of the curve and maintain a competitive edge in their respective industries.

3. Adapting to Remote Work: The rise of remote work in recent years has further underscored the importance of adaptability in workflow management. Traditional workflows designed for in-person collaboration may not be well-suited to remote work environments, where team members are geographically dispersed and communication channels may be less formal. Adjusting workflows to accommodate remote work requires careful consideration of factors such as communication protocols, project management tools, and performance metrics.

Practical Strategies for Adjusting Workflows Accordingly:

Mindful Productivity: Cultivating Quality Work, Achieving balance and Sustainable Habits for Lasting Success

With the need for adaptability firmly established, let's explore some practical strategies for adjusting workflows to ensure optimal productivity:

1. Conduct Regular Workflow Audits:Regularly auditing workflows is essential for identifying areas that may need adjustment. This involves analyzing each step of a workflow to identify inefficiencies, redundancies, and bottlenecks. By conducting these audits on a regular basis, organizations can proactively identify areas for improvement and implement changes to enhance efficiency.

2. Seek Input from Stakeholders:When adjusting workflows, it's important to seek input from stakeholders who will be affected by the changes. This may include team members, managers, clients, and other relevant parties. By involving stakeholders in the decision-making process, organizations can gain valuable insights and ensure that changes are implemented smoothly and effectively.

3. Embrace Agile Methodologies:Agile methodologies such as Scrum and Kanban are

well-suited to environments where adaptability is paramount. These methodologies emphasize iterative development, continuous improvement, and collaboration, making them ideal for adjusting workflows in response to changing priorities and requirements. By embracing agile principles, organizations can foster a culture of adaptability and innovation that enables them to thrive in a rapidly changing world.

4. Invest in Training and Development: Adjusting workflows often requires employees to learn new skills or adapt to new processes. Investing in training and development programs can help ensure that employees have the knowledge and resources they need to succeed in a changing environment. Whether it's providing access to online courses, hosting workshops, or offering one-on-one coaching, organizations can empower employees to embrace change and thrive in dynamic work environments.

5. Monitor Performance Metrics: Monitoring performance metrics is essential for evaluating the effectiveness of adjusted workflows. By tracking key performance indicators such as

Mindful Productivity: Cultivating Quality Work, Achieving balance and Sustainable Habits for Lasting Success

productivity, efficiency, and customer satisfaction, organizations can gauge the impact of changes and make further adjustments as needed. This continuous feedback loop allows organizations to fine-tune workflows over time, ensuring that they remain aligned with strategic objectives and deliver optimal results.

Case Studies in Workflow Adaptability:

To illustrate the importance of adaptability in workflow management, let's explore some real-world case studies of organizations that have successfully adjusted their workflows to meet changing needs:

1. Netflix: Netflix is a prime example of a company that has embraced adaptability in its workflow management practices. As the streaming landscape has evolved, Netflix has continuously adjusted its workflows to stay ahead of the competition. This includes everything from developing new algorithms to personalize recommendations for users to investing in original content production to differentiate its platform from competitors. By remaining agile and responsive to changing

market dynamics, Netflix has maintained its position as a leader in the streaming industry.

2. Slack:Slack is another company that has prioritized adaptability in its workflow management approach. As a provider of team communication and collaboration tools, Slack understands the importance of staying agile in a rapidly changing market. The company regularly solicits feedback from users and uses this input to make adjustments to its product roadmap and development processes. This iterative approach allows Slack to continuously improve its platform and deliver new features and functionalities that meet the evolving needs of its users

In conclusion, adjusting workflows accordingly is essential for maintaining productivity and achieving success in today's dynamic work environment. By recognizing the need for adaptability and implementing practical strategies for adjusting workflows, organizations can stay ahead of the curve and deliver optimal results. Whether it's responding to changing priorities, embracing technological

Mindful Productivity: Cultivating Quality Work, Achieving balance and Sustainable Habits for Lasting Success

advancements, or adapting to remote work, organizations that prioritize adaptability in workflow management are better positioned to thrive in a rapidly changing world.

Mindful Productivity: Cultivating Quality Work, Achieving balance and Sustainable Habits for Lasting Success

Chapter 7.

Shifting Towards Long-Term Quality:

Prioritizing Sustainability and Excellence in Work and LifeThere is a growing awareness of the significance of moving away from a focus on short-term quality and toward long-term quality in a world that frequently prioritizes speed and quantity above depth and quality. Long-term happiness and success can result from placing a higher priority on sustainability and excellence, whether in our professional lives, interpersonal relationships, or personal endeavors. We will examine the idea of moving toward long-term quality in this thorough guide, looking at its advantages, difficulties, and workable implementation options.

Recognizing the Value of Long-Term Quality

It's simple to get sucked into the chase of quick fixes and short-term profits in today's fast-paced environment. Messages telling us to do more, do more, and get more are all around us, frequently at the sacrifice of sustainability and quality. But

Mindful Productivity: Cultivating Quality Work, Achieving balance and Sustainable Habits for Lasting Success

studies have indicated that putting long-term quality ahead of short-term quantity might ultimately result in higher levels of achievement, resilience, and pleasure.

1. Sustainability: Moving toward long-term quality has many advantages, one of which is sustainability. We can design longer-lasting, more sustainable systems and processes by putting quality before quantity. This holds true for both personal and professional habits. Rather than pursuing ephemeral gains or transient joys, we should concentrate on laying strong foundations that will sustain us in the long run and increase our stability and ability to overcome obstacles.

2. Excellence is yet another important advantage of putting long-term quality first. We can attain a greater degree of excellence in both our work and life when we make the commitment to doing things properly rather than just finishing them quickly. This holds true for both solitary and group pursuits. By aiming for excellence in all we do, we can foster an excellence-driven culture that encourages others to follow suit,

resulting in increased success, innovation, and creativity.

3. *Fulfillment: Putting long-term quality first can, arguably most critically, increase our level of fulfillment and contentment in life. We feel proud and accomplished of our work when we take the time to complete tasks correctly. The pursuit of long-term quality can profoundly improve our lives, whether it is by reaching our full potential on a project, cultivating meaningful relationships, or tenaciously following our passions.

Effective Techniques for Transitioning to Long-Term Quality:

After seeing the significance of making the transition to long-term quality, let's look at some doable tactics for putting this philosophy into practice in both our personal and professional lives:

1. Establish Meaningful Goals: Invest some time in creating long-term, meaningful goals that are consistent with your values and aspirations rather than concentrating only on short-term objectives or results. These could include

Mindful Productivity: Cultivating Quality Work, Achieving balance and Sustainable Habits for Lasting Success

objectives for developing personally, advancing professionally, or having a constructive influence on the community. You can stay focused on the big picture and keep away from temporary distractions by defining clear, relevant goals.

2. Develop Patience and Persistence: It takes both of these qualities to make the transition to long-term quality. It's critical to understand that real change requires time and work, and to maintain your commitment to your objectives in the face of setbacks or slow progress. Develop a resilient and persistent mindset, and have faith that your efforts will ultimately be rewarded.

3. Relationship Prioritization: It's simple to put efficiency and productivity before of deep connections in our fast-paced society. On the other hand, sustaining solid, healthy relationships is crucial to long-term happiness. Allocate time for significant interactions with friends, family, and coworkers, and make a sustained effort to cultivate and uphold such bonds. Recall that building strong connections

requires time and work, but the benefits are ultimately priceless.

4. Put Your Attention on Constant Improvement: Put your attention on making both your work and your life better rather than aiming for perfection. Adopt a growth attitude and see obstacles and setbacks as chances for improvement. Seek input from others, think back on your experiences, and always look for methods to improve your abilities, knowledge, and skills. You may steadily increase both the quality of your life and the quality of your work over time by making continuous improvement a priority.

5. Practice Presence and Mindfulness: Lastly, incorporate presence and mindfulness into your everyday activities. Rather than working quickly through assignments or continuously juggling multiple projects at once, give your current task your whole attention. Develop an appreciation for the richness of every experience, whether it is when working on a project, enjoying a meal, or spending time with loved ones. You may improve the quality of your life overall and

Mindful Productivity: Cultivating Quality Work, Achieving balance and Sustainable Habits for Lasting Success

strengthen your connection to the present moment by engaging in mindfulness and presence practices.

Case Studies Regarding Durable Quality:

To demonstrate the advantages of adopting a long-term quality-focused mindset, let's examine some actual case studies of people and businesses who have done so successfully:

1. Toyota: One of the best examples of a business that puts long-term quality first in its operations is Toyota. The Toyota Production System (TPS), which is the company's production system, is well-known for emphasizing employee empowerment, waste reduction, and continual development. As a result of putting quality above quantity and making long-lasting investments in systems and procedures, Toyota has grown to become one of the most reputable and prosperous automakers in the world.

2. Warren Buffett: Known for his patient and long-term approach to investment, Warren Buffett is regarded as one of the all-time great investors. Buffett concentrates on discovering

Mindful Productivity: Cultivating Quality Work, Achieving balance and Sustainable Habits for Lasting Success

high-quality companies with good fundamentals and hanging onto them for the long term, as opposed to pursuing short-term gains or trying to time the market. Over several decades, Buffett has consistently and sustainably generated returns for himself and his investors by placing a higher priority on long-term quality than on short-term profits.

In summary, making the transition to long-term quality is critical to attaining long-term success and fulfillment in both the professional and personal spheres. We may build long-lasting lives and organizations by putting sustainability, excellence, and fulfillment above quick money and fast satisfaction. There are numerous useful ways to incorporate this attitude into our daily lives, such as practicing mindfulness and presence, prioritizing relationships, building patience and tenacity, making meaningful goals, or concentrating on continual progress. We can build a more meaningful, contented, and sustainable future for ourselves and future generations if we adopt the long-term quality attitude.

Mindful Productivity: Cultivating Quality Work, Achieving balance and Sustainable Habits for Lasting Success

Establishing Durable Routines: An All-Inclusive Handbook for Prolonged Achievement and Welfare

Our daily lives are constructed by our habits, which influence our attitudes, behaviors, and results. While many of us work hard to form virtuous habits that help us achieve our objectives, maintaining these behaviors over time can be very difficult. We will examine the idea of creating long-lasting habits in this thorough book, looking at the advantages of doing so, the science underlying habit development, and doable tactics for creating enduring habits.

Recognizing the Value of Sustainable Behaviors

Habits that we can sustain over time and that improve our general well-being, productivity, and health are known as sustainable habits. Sustainable habits are based on constancy, tenacity, and intentionality as opposed to passing fads or fast cures. Long-term positive changes in our lives as well as increased success and fulfillment can be attained by developing enduring habits.

1. Consistency is one of the main advantages of durable behaviors. A behavior becomes established in our daily routine and needs less conscious effort to maintain when we engage in it consistently over time. Developing consistent behaviors increases the likelihood of positive results and long-lasting improvement in our relationships, careers, and health.

2. Stability: We get a sense of predictability and stability in our life when we adopt sustainable behaviors. We may create a feeling of structure and order that can help lessen stress and anxiety by instituting regular rituals and routines. Increased sentiments of contentment and well-being can be attributed to having control over our everyday activities and knowing what to expect.

3. Long-Term Outcomes: Probably most significantly, long-term outcomes are the product of durable habits. Consistent practices can have long-term benefits, even though they might not become apparent right away. Building

meaningful connections, learning a new skill, or losing weight are all examples of sustainable behaviors that set the stage for long-term success and wellbeing.

The Study of Habit Formation Science:

It's useful to investigate the science of habit formation in order to comprehend how to create long-lasting habits. Cue, routine, and reward are the three main elements of "habit loops," which are the processes by which habits are created.

1. Cue: A cue is an external stimulus that initiates a behavior. It might be a certain day, a certain place, or a certain emotional state. For instance, seeing a yoga mat may cue the habit of practicing yoga, whereas feeling anxious may activate the habit of stress-eating.

2. Routine: The behavior itself, or the response to the signal, is what we refer to as routine. This might involve everything from browsing social media to running to practicing meditation.

3. Reward: The good thing that happens to us or the emotion we get from the behavior is the reward. It could be a physical experience like

pleasure or relief, a sense of accomplishment, or a sense of rest.

Realistic Techniques for Creating Durable Habits:

Now that we know the value of long-lasting habits and the principles underlying habit development, let's look at some doable methods for creating enduring habits:

1. Start Small: It's critical to begin small when forming sustainable habits and to build momentum gradually over time. Instead of attempting to make big changes all at once, concentrate on coming up with doable, incremental steps that you can take on a regular basis. If your objective is to exercise more, for instance, begin with a daily stroll and work your way up to longer and more intense workouts as your confidence and consistency grow.

2. Establish Specific Goals: To give your habit-building efforts focus and inspiration, precisely identify your goals and objectives. To improve your chances of success, set SMART (specific, measurable, achievable, relevant, and time-bound) goals. Rather than aiming for

something general like "get in shape," for instance, make your objective more focused like "run a 5K race in three months."

3. Establish a Habit Loop: Assemble a habit loop by associating your desired behavior with a particular cue and reward in order to form enduring habits. Determine the cue that sets off the behavior you wish to develop, plan an action or routine to respond to the cue, and decide on a reward for yourself when you accomplish the behavior. If your objective is to increase your water intake, for instance, you may set a phone reminder (trigger), have a glass of water (habit), and treat yourself to a feeling of hydration and wellbeing (reward).

4. Use Implementation Intentions: Preliminary plans that assist you in carrying out your desired behavior in particular circumstances are known as implementation intentions. Implementation goals can greatly improve the likelihood that you will carry out your objectives, according to research. Make a detailed strategy for the times, locations, and methods of your exercise, for instance, rather than just deciding to exercise

more. This could be making workout appointments on your calendar, preparing your gym bag the night before, or finding a workout partner who will hold you responsible.

5. Track Your Progress: Keep tabs on your behaviors and pinpoint areas that need work by tracking your progress on a regular basis. To document your everyday actions and reflect on your accomplishments and setbacks, keep a notebook or habit tracker. Celebrate your accomplishments and learn from losses to improve your strategy and modify your habits as necessary.

Case Studies on Creating Sustainable Habits:

Let's look at some real-world case studies of people who have successfully developed enduring habits to highlight the advantages of doing so.

1. James Clear: James Clear is the best-selling author of "Atomic Habits," a book that delves into the science of habit development and offers doable tactics for creating enduring habits. In order to maximize the chances of new habits succeeding, Clear's method highlights the value

Mindful Productivity: Cultivating Quality Work, Achieving balance and Sustainable Habits for Lasting Success

of making little, gradual adjustments as well as the effectiveness of habit stacking. Through the use of the concepts presented in his book, Clear has assisted a great number of people in changing their behaviors and realizing their objectives.

2. Marie Kondo: Marie Kondo is a well-known organizational expert and the author of the best-selling book "The Life-Changing Magic of Tidying Up." She emphasizes simplicity and decluttering in order to foster harmony and order in one's surroundings. Through her guidance on how to develop the routine of routinely organizing one's space and parting with items that no longer provide happiness, Marie Kondo has enabled millions of people to design homes and lives that reflect their goals and values.

Developing long-lasting habits is crucial to success and happiness in the long run, at work and in life. Consistency, stability, and long-term results are important, and by putting them first, we can develop enduring habits that benefit both us and people around us. There are numerous doable tactics for developing long-lasting habits, such as measuring progress, utilizing implementation intents, starting small, defining specific goals, and building habit loops. We can design lives that are meaningful, purposeful, and incredibly gratifying by putting these techniques into practice and adopting the sustainable habit building attitude.

Unleashing Creativity and Innovation: An All-Inclusive Manual for Promoting Development and Change

Innovation and creativity are what propel development and change in all spheres of our existence, including business, technology, and the arts and cultures. However, a lot of us find it difficult to express our creativity and realize original ideas. We will examine the idea of encouraging creativity and innovation in this extensive book, looking at the advantages of adopting a creative mentality, the obstacles to creativity, and doable tactics for developing our creative potential and bringing about significant change.

Recognizing the Value of Innovation and Creativity

In today's world of rapid change, creativity and innovation are critical for finding solutions to complicated challenges, embracing change, and advancing society. Creativity and innovation are the engines of growth and change, whether they are employed in the development of ground-breaking technologies, the production of moving artwork, or the rethinking of established business strategies. Individuals and organizations can open up new possibilities, motivate others, and have a long-lasting effect on the world by encouraging creativity and innovation.

1. Problem-Solving: Overcoming obstacles and resolving complicated issues require creativity and inventiveness. When we tackle problems creatively, we can come up with original answers, think beyond the box, and discover fresh approaches to problems that have baffled others. The key to bringing about significant change and improving the world is creativity and invention, whether the goal is treating social

inequity, creating sustainable energy sources, or curing sickness.

2. Adaptability: More than ever, adaptability is crucial in the fast-paced world of today. Innovation and creativity help people and organizations remain ahead of the curve, take advantage of new opportunities, and adjust to changing conditions. We can thrive in the face of uncertainty and move confidently and nimbly through the intricacies of the modern world by adopting a creative mentality and encouraging an innovative culture.

3. Inspiration: We are motivated to dream large, think creatively, and push the envelope of what is conceivable via creativity and innovation. Creativity and innovation have the ability to uplift and inspire us, kindling our passions and sparking our imaginations, whether we are witnessing the beauty of a beautiful piece of art, marveling at the cleverness of a remarkable invention, or feeling the rush of a revolutionary new idea.

The Obstacles to Originality:

Even though creativity and innovation are important, many of us find it difficult to use our creative potential and implement novel ideas. There are a number of typical obstacles to creativity that can impair our capacity for original thought and the development of novel solutions:

1. Fear of Failure: The fear of failure is one of the biggest obstacles to innovation. For fear of failing or being rejected, a lot of us are scared to take chances, make errors, or go outside of our comfort zones. This anxiety has the power to inhibit our creativity and keep us from trying out novel concepts or methods that might result in ground-breaking inventions.

2. Perfectionism: Another prevalent obstacle to creativity is perfectionism. When we hold ourselves to an impossible standard and aim for excellence in all we do, we risk becoming immobilized by uncertainty and indecision. Rather of welcoming experimentation and imperfection, we could get obsessed with doing

things perfectly, which would result in stagnation and lost chances for creativity.

3. Lack of Time: Many of us find it difficult to find the time and space necessary for original thought and invention in the fast-paced world of today. There is little time for introspection, research, or experimenting because we are inundated with interruptions, deadlines, and demands on our time. Our capacity for innovation may remain unrealized and our capacity to effect significant change may be constrained in the absence of time and space set aside for creativity.

Effective Methods for Promoting Innovation and Creativity:

Thankfully, there exist numerous pragmatic approaches to surmount these obstacles to creativity and cultivate an innovative culture:

1. Develop a Growth Mindset: A growth mindset is the conviction that our skills and intelligence can be enhanced by hard work and persistence. Consider failure an opportunity for learning and development rather than a setback. You can get over your fear of failing and see experimentation

and taking risks as vital steps in the creative process by developing a growth mindset.

2. Establish a Safe and Supportive Environment: Encourage the creation of a safe and encouraging environment where people are encouraged to voice their opinions, take chances, and question the status quo. Promote candid dialogue, teamwork, and helpful criticism, and acknowledge both achievements and setbacks as worthwhile educational opportunities. You can unlock the full creative potential of your team and cultivate an innovative attitude that propels significant change by establishing a culture of psychological safety.

3. Promote Divergent Thinking: Promote Divergent thinking, the capacity to come up with several, unique solutions to an issue. Encourage people to welcome ambiguity and uncertainty, try out many strategies, and investigate a broad range of options rather than looking for the "right" answer. Divergent thinking can help you discover fresh viewpoints, insights, and concepts that could result in ground-breaking inventions.

4. Offer Opportunities for Research and Experimentation: Offer chances for research and experimentation, both individually and in groups. Urge people to engage in creative endeavors, follow their passions, and discover new interests outside of their regular obligations. Provide areas for teams to interact, brainstorm, and prototype new ideas during design thinking workshops, innovation labs, and brainstorming sessions. You can encourage creativity and innovation across your company by giving people the chance to explore and try new things.

5. Lastly, set an example for others to follow by committing to originality and innovation in your own job.

Chapter 8

Unlocking Success: Practical Strategies for Implementation

focuses on putting plans and ideas into practice by using workable implementation tactics. The ability to generate new ideas and solutions requires creativity and invention, but the real test of success is how well we can put those ideas into practice. This chapter will cover a range of useful tactics and methods for realizing goals, conquering everyday obstacles, and producing observable outcomes.

Creating the Conditions for Success:

Establishing alignment, clarity, and commitment among stakeholders is crucial to success before delving into particular implementation tactics. This includes:

1. Clarifying Goals: Clearly state the goals and expected results of the project or endeavor. Make sure that all parties are aware of the goal, parameters, and anticipated outcomes.

2. Assigning Roles and duties: Assign team members roles and duties so that everyone is

aware of what is expected of them and how their contributions affect the project's success as a whole.

3. Making a Plan: Create a thorough implementation plan that specifies the actions, deadlines, and materials needed to accomplish the goals. Divide the strategy into doable tasks and deadlines, and set up systems for monitoring development and adjusting course as necessary.

Let's now examine several doable tactics for effective implementation:

1EffectiveCommunication:Implementation success depends on effective communication. Throughout the process, keep stakeholders informed and involved by giving them regular updates on the status of the project, responding to any worries or inquiries, and asking for their opinions. Make use of a range of communication channels to make sure that information is shared openly and transparently, including emails, meetings, and project management software.

2. **Prioritize and Sequence Tasks:** To increase productivity and reduce delays, prioritize tasks according to their urgency and

importance. Then, arrange them logically in order of increasing importance. Prioritize finishing important activities first, taking into account task dependencies and interdependencies. To guarantee that deadlines are fulfilled, divide more complex activities into smaller, easier-to-manage subtasks and assign resources appropriately.

3. **Manage Risks:** Recognize possible risks and uncertainties that might affect the implementation effort's success, and create plans for successfully reducing or managing them. To address possible risks, this may entail creating backup plans, risk assessments, and resource allocation. As dangers and problems emerge, take the initiative to handle them and maintain an open, flexible, and adaptive mindset.

4. **Empower and Motivate Teams:** Give your teams the tools, encouragement, and independence they require to be successful. Promote originality, ingenuity, and problem-solving skills while honoring and commemorating small victories and significant turning points. Encourage a climate of

cooperation, responsibility, and trust so that team members feel appreciated, respected, and motivated to put forth their best work.

5. **Monitor and Evaluate Progress:** To keep the project on schedule, continuously monitor and assess progress in relation to the implementation plan, keeping track of milestones and key performance indicators. Review and evaluate strategy and tactics on a regular basis, and adapt as necessary to overcome obstacles or seize opportunities. Get input from team members and stakeholders, then utilize it to guide choices and promote ongoing development.

6. **Celebrate Success and Learn from Failure:** Highlight accomplishments and significant junctures along the implementation process, acknowledging the laborious efforts and valuable input of all those engaged. Likewise, see mistakes and disappointments as chances for development and learning rather than as insurmountable roadblocks. Review the implementation process after it has been completed to find best practices and lessons

learned that may be used to upcoming projects and endeavors.

Thorough planning, clear communication, proactive risk management, and capable leadership are necessary for successful execution. Organizations may translate their vision into reality and produce significant outcomes by adhering to workable implementation strategies and cultivating a culture of cooperation, creativity, and accountability. In order to overcome obstacles and grasp possibilities, always remember to be adaptive and flexible, and be ready to change course when necessary. Everything is achievable with the correct attitude and strategy.

Time Blocking Techniques: A Comprehensive Guide to Increasing Productivity

Being productive is crucial to reaching our objectives and making the most of our time in a world where there are many distractions and demands on our time. Time blocking is a highly effective method for increasing productivity and taking back control of our calendars. We'll go over the idea of time blocking, its advantages, and useful methods for putting it into practice to increase your output and efficiency in this article.

Comprehending Time Blocking:

As a time management strategy, time blocking entails allocating particular time slots for various assignments, pursuits, or priorities. By planning your day in advance and setting aside specific time to concentrate on your most critical tasks, time blocking helps you avoid depending on a to-do list or responding to interruptions and requests. You may reduce distractions, improve attention, and move closer to your goals more quickly by planning your day into blocks of time allocated to particular chores or projects.

The advantages of time blocking

Numerous advantages of time blocking can help you increase your effectiveness and productivity in both your personal and professional lives:

1. **Better Focus and Concentration:** You can reduce distractions and focus entirely on the subject at hand by setting up uninterrupted time blocks for particular tasks or projects. By doing this, you can enter a state of flow when your

Mindful Productivity: Cultivating Quality Work, Achieving balance and Sustainable Habits for Lasting Success

productivity, attention, and level of concentration are all increased.

2. **Better Planning and Prioritization:** Setting time blocks compels you to set priorities for your tasks and allot time to those that fit your objectives and top priorities. You may make sure that your energies are being directed toward the things that will have the biggest impact by organizing your day ahead of time and allotting time for crucial chores.

3. **Better Time Management:** By giving your day structure and regularity, time blocking enables you to manage your time more effectively. You may prevent overcommitting, minimize procrastination, and maximize the use of your free time by segmenting your day into discrete time slots for various tasks.

4. **Increased Productivity and Efficiency:** Time blocking can help you work more productively and complete more tasks in less time by discouraging multitasking and focusing on one activity at a time. You can achieve more in a day and move closer to your goals by setting out time for particular chores.

Useful Methods for Scheduling Time:

After discussing the advantages of time blocking, let's look at some useful methods for putting it into practice:

1. **Determine Your Priorities:** To begin, list your top objectives and priorities for the coming day, week, or month. Which jobs or projects need the most attention right now? You can assign time blocks in accordance with your priorities once you have a firm grasp on them.

2. **Make a Schedule:** Break your day, week, or month down into time blocks by using a calendar or planner to make a schedule. Establish time blocks for non-negotiable commitments, like appointments, meetings, and personal duties. Next, set up certain time slots to concentrate on your most critical assignments or projects.

3. **Set Time Limits:** Depending on the difficulty and urgency of the activity, allocate a set amount of time to each time block. This makes you feel more accountable and driven, which helps you stay concentrated and productive during each block of time.

Mindful Productivity: Cultivating Quality Work, Achieving balance and Sustainable Habits for Lasting Success

4. **Group Similar Tasks** Assign similar tasks or activities to a group and set aside a specific amount of time to work on them at a time. Set up time on your calendar, for instance, to answer emails, make phone calls, and engage in creative or brainstorming activities. By doing this, you may decrease context switches and increase productivity.

5. **Protect Your Time:** After you've set aside time for particular projects or pursuits, treat that period of time as you would a meeting or appointment. To reduce distractions, don't plan other obligations or allow interruptions during specific time slots. Also, let people know when you're available.

6. **Be Flexible:** Although time blocking offers regularity and structure, it's crucial to maintain your flexibility and adaptability. There may be unforeseen circumstances or crises that call for last-minute scheduling adjustments. Be ready to reorganize your time blocks as necessary to account for shifting demands or situations.

7. **Review and Adjust:** Review your time blocking plan on a regular basis to evaluate your progress and pinpoint areas that need work. Do you give your main priorities enough of your time? Are there any jobs or activities that could be assigned to someone else or stopped completely? Utilize this input to modify your time blocking strategy and gradually improve your schedule.

Time blocking is a highly effective strategy for improving focus, productivity, and goal achievement. You can reduce distractions, maximize your time, and complete more work in less time by strategically organizing your day and setting out time for your most crucial tasks. Try out various time blocking strategies to see which one suits you the most. Then, observe how your productivity increases and your objectives become more attainable.

Accepting Digital Minimalism: Regaining Concentration in a Distracted World

Our attention spans can easily be overwhelmed by the constant onslaught of emails, social media updates, and notifications in today's

Mindful Productivity: Cultivating Quality Work, Achieving balance and Sustainable Habits for Lasting Success

hyperconnected society, leaving us feeling disoriented and unfocused. Here comes the concept of "digital minimalism," which promotes the deliberate and thoughtful use of technology to help us regain our concentration and lead more fulfilling lives.

Digital minimalism is essentially about simplifying our digital life by identifying the most important things to prioritize and carefully considering the role that technology plays in our day-to-day activities. Digital minimalists manage their online experiences to reflect their ideals and objectives, as opposed to simply ingesting information or continually browsing through feeds.

One of the main tenets of digital minimalism is "less is more." We may focus on greater engagement and concentration by minimizing the amount of apps, subscriptions, and digital distractions competing for our attention. This may be removing pointless apps, stopping email newsletter subscriptions, or establishing limits on how much time is spent on a gadget.

Mindful Productivity: Cultivating Quality Work, Achieving balance and Sustainable Habits for Lasting Success

Digital minimalism, however, does not advocate giving up on technology completely. Rather, it motivates us to take a more thoughtful and conscientious approach to our online behaviors. This could entail putting ideas into practice like digital detoxes, in which we step away from screens for a while in order to refuel and get back in touch with the real world.

Digital minimalism's fundamental goal is to help us take back control of our attention and develop clarity and focus in the face of the digital age's cacophony. We may create a more balanced and meaningful life by deliberately selecting how we use technology and giving tasks that make us happy and fulfilled priority.

Digital minimalism is really about taking back our attention and focus in a world where there are always competing demands on it. It goes beyond simply cutting down on screen time or streamlining our digital gadgets. We can develop a stronger sense of presence, purpose, and fulfillment in our lives by adopting the digital minimalist tenets.

Mindful Productivity: Cultivating Quality Work, Achieving balance and Sustainable Habits for Lasting Success

Developing Mindfulness to Foster Work-Life Balance: Achieving Harmony in a hectic World

Finding a healthy balance between work obligations and personal time can seem like an impossible task in the hectic and fast-paced workplace of today. But mindfulness offers a potent remedy for the never-ending clamor, offering a means to become more present, aware, and balanced in both work and life.

Fundamentally, mindfulness involves intentionally focusing attention on the current moment while letting go of judgment. We can develop a greater feeling of clarity, resilience, and inner calm by fully observing our thoughts, emotions, and sensations as they arise. These traits are important for navigating the difficulties of modern life.

Mindfulness is a fundamental tool for stress management, improving focus, and cultivating better contentment and pleasure in both personal and professional spheres when it comes to work-life balance. Here are some ways that

Mindful Productivity: Cultivating Quality Work, Achieving balance and Sustainable Habits for Lasting Success

mindfulness might lead to a life that is more balanced and harmonious:

1. Stress Reduction: By encouraging relaxation and soothing the nervous system, mindfulness techniques including body scans, deep breathing exercises, and meditation can help lower stress levels. We can face challenges with more poise and resilience if we get a better understanding of our stress triggers and reactions.

2. Increased Productivity and Focus: Mindfulness techniques help us pay attention and focus better, which makes it possible for us to operate more productively and efficiently. We may reduce distractions and do more tasks in less time by teaching our thoughts to stay present and focused on the task at hand. This will free us more time for leisure and relaxation.

3. Better Relationships: Being mindful helps cultivate increased emotional intelligence, empathy, and compassion—qualities that are crucial for creating enduring bonds with people at home and at work. Deep listening techniques and a nonjudgmental mindset can help us

Mindful Productivity: Cultivating Quality Work, Achieving balance and Sustainable Habits for Lasting Success

improve our ability to collaborate, communicate, and resolve conflicts in all facets of our lives.

4. Setting limits: Mindfulness gives us the ability to prioritize self-care and set appropriate limits, both of which are crucial for preserving a work-life balance. We may set clear guidelines for work hours, responsibilities, and technology use by being aware of our own needs and values. This will help us make time and energy available for activities that will nourish and revitalize us.

5. Joy and Gratitude: Mindfulness helps us discover joy and fulfillment in both work and leisure pursuits by fostering an attitude of appreciation and gratitude for the present moment. We may combat the need to always aim for more and develop a stronger sense of happiness and well-being by appreciating life's small joys and counting our blessings.

Mindfulness is a potent technique that helps us achieve work-life balance by encouraging more intentionality, awareness, and presence in our daily lives. We may lower stress, sharpen our attention, strengthen our relationships, establish healthy boundaries, and experience more joy and

Mindful Productivity: Cultivating Quality Work, Achieving balance and Sustainable Habits for Lasting Success

fulfillment in our work and personal lives by implementing mindfulness techniques into our daily lives.

Chapter 9.

Overcoming Resistance: Navigating Challenges and Unlocking Success

An unavoidable aspect of the human experience is resistance. We run against roadblocks, failures, and internal opposition while we're trying to achieve substantial transformation, career success, or personal improvement. We'll go further into the idea of resistance in this thorough examination, looking at its many manifestations, typical problems that crop up, and useful tactics for getting over resistance and succeeding.

Comprehending Opposition:
There are many different external and internal ways that resistance might appear. Institutional hurdles, other people's resistance, and society standards are a few examples of the causes of external resistance. Conversely, internal opposition stems from our own uncertainties, anxieties, and limiting beliefs. Whatever its origin, resistance frequently manifests in

emotions that prevent us from acting and pursuing our objectives, such as fear, self-doubt, procrastination, or lethargy.

Typical Problems and Their Fixes:

1. Fear of Failure: - Challenge: One of the most common types of resistance is fear of failing. The idea of making errors or not living up to our standards paralyzes a lot of us, which results in avoidance habits and lost chances.

   - Solution: Reframing failure as a normal aspect of learning and a chance for personal development is essential to overcoming the fear of failure. Adopt a growth mentality, acknowledge and appreciate accomplishments, and see failures as opportunities for personal growth.

2. Self-Doubt: - Challenge: Self-doubt makes us less confident in our skills and abilities, which makes us reluctant to work toward our objectives.

   - Resolve self-doubt by developing a positive self-image and engaging in self-compassion exercises. In order to overcome negative thoughts and beliefs, concentrate on your accomplishments and strengths, and look for support from positive people who have faith in your skills.

3. Procrastination: - Challenge: Driven by the need for instant gratification and the need to avoid discomfort, procrastination is a frequent coping method for handling opposition.

 - Solution: Get rid of procrastination by dividing work into smaller, more manageable chunks, establishing deadlines, and setting up a conducive environment that encourages concentration and production. Create rituals and habits to tell your brain when it's time to work.

4. The Aim for Perfection:

 - Difficulty: Perfectionism creates unreasonably high expectations, which paralyze people and prevent them from acting out of fear of not measuring up.

 - Solution: Overcome perfectionism by accepting imperfection and seeing failures as chances for improvement. Establish reasonable objectives, prioritize progress over perfection, and acknowledge that even a little activity is better than none at all.

5. Lack of Motivation: - Difficulty: When we lack motivation, it can be exhausting and difficult to find the will to work toward our objectives.

- Rekindle motivation by reminding yourself of the significance of your objectives and reestablishing a connection with your values and passions. Establish attainable, relevant goals that are in line with your dreams, acknowledge your accomplishments, and get motivation from people who have surmounted comparable obstacles.

Effective Techniques for Overcoming Opposition:

Apart from tackling particular obstacles, a few useful techniques can assist in surmounting reluctance and advancing our progress:

1. Self-awareness and mindfulness:

- Develop self-awareness and mindfulness to identify resistance and comprehend its root causes. We can gain more understanding of our patterns of resistance by objectively monitoring our thoughts and feelings.

2. Planning and Setting Goals:

- Establish measurable objectives and create workable methods to attain them. To track progress and ensure responsibility, break down goals into smaller, more doable steps and set deadlines.

3. Positive Affirmations and Visualization: Rewire limiting beliefs and visualize success by using positive affirmations and visualization techniques. Reframing negative self-talk with affirmations and mentally practicing success and confidence-boosting visualizations are two effective strategies.

4. Accountability and Assistance: - Seek assistance and accountability from dependable friends, mentors, or coaches who can offer accountability, motivation, and direction. Talk to people about your objectives and advancements to get their support in staying inspired and on course.

5. Resilience and Adaptability: - Develop these qualities to help you overcome obstacles and setbacks along the path. Consider setbacks as chances for personal development and have a flexible mindset, adapting your tactics to get

Mindful Productivity: Cultivating Quality Work, Achieving balance and Sustainable Habits for Lasting Success

beyond setbacks and maintain focus on your objectives.

Although resistance is an unavoidable element of the path to achievement, it doesn't have to stop us. We can overcome obstacles, realize our potential, and accomplish our objectives by comprehending the different types of resistance, identifying typical difficulties, and putting into practice workable techniques for doing so. Accept the road, develop resilience, and never forget that each challenge we face moves us one step closer to realizing our goals.

Chapter 10

Embracing Slow Productivity: Cultivating Fulfillment and Success in a Fast-Paced World

The goal of productivity in today's fast-paced world frequently centers on completing tasks in less time. Messages that exalt hustling culture and stress the value of perpetual busyness are all around us. Nevertheless, our happiness and sense of fulfillment may suffer as a result of this unwavering emphasis on efficiency and speed. We will dive into the idea of slow productivity in this in-depth analysis, looking at its advantages, guiding principles, and useful tactics for adopting a more purposeful and happy lifestyle at work and in life.

Comprehending Slow Productivity

The concept of slow productivity refutes the widely held belief that productivity is limited to accomplishing more tasks in less time. Rather, it highlights the significance of working at a natural pace, giving quality precedence over quantity, and developing a more profound sense of purpose and joy in both our work and personal life. Fundamentally, slow productivity is about taking back our time and priorities, as well as rejecting the culture of activity.

Advantages of Slow Production:

1. Improved Well-Being: Slow productivity lowers stress and burnout by allowing workers to work at their own speed without feeling pressured to achieve more. It enables us to place a higher priority on relaxation, self-care, and sleep, which promotes better mental and physical health.

2. Enhanced Creativity: Slow productivity gives creativity more room and leeway to grow. We may unlock our creative potential and produce original ideas and solutions by giving ourselves permission to slow down and work intently.

3. Better Relationships: When productivity is poor, we are more inclined to value deep ties and relationships over fleeting exchanges. Our personal and professional lives can be more fulfilling and satisfying if we devote time and

Mindful Productivity: Cultivating Quality Work, Achieving balance and Sustainable Habits for Lasting Success

effort to establishing and maintaining relationships.

4. Greater Focus and Effectiveness: Slow productivity highlights the value of focus and effectiveness in contrast to the notion that productivity is only about speed. We may do better in less time and with less effort if we work thoughtfully and purposefully.

The fundamentals of slow productivity

1. Perform Fewer Tasks: Slow productivity promotes performing fewer tasks with excellence. Rather than overcommitting ourselves to a few high-impact projects that are consistent with our objectives and beliefs, we concentrate on a select number of these projects.

2. operate at Your Own Pace: Slow productivity motivates us to operate at a speed that suits our needs and is sustainable. Instead of working frantically to fulfill pointless deadlines, we give ourselves the time and space to do tasks deliberately and systematically.

3. Obsess over Quality: Slow productivity results from a preference for quality over quantity. We work hard to create work of the

Mindful Productivity: Cultivating Quality Work, Achieving balance and Sustainable Habits for Lasting Success

best quality by focusing on the little things, honing our skills, and never stopping looking for ways to do better.

Useful Techniques for Adapting to Slow Productivity:

1. Set Reasonable Expectations: Don't overcommit yourself and be reasonable about what you can achieve in a certain amount of time. Adequately utilize your time and energy by concentrating on a small number of top priorities.

2. Engage in Mindful Work: Develop mindfulness at work by giving each task your complete attention and concentrating on it one at a time. Reduce the amount of outside noise and interruptions, and give your whole attention to the here and now.

3. Plan Regular Breaks: Include times during the day for relaxation and rejuvenation. Take quick strolls, work on your deep breathing, or partake in relaxing and joyful hobbies.

4. Limit Multitasking: Since multitasking splits our attention and impairs our capacity to concentrate, it is the opposite of sluggish

productivity. Rather, concentrate on finishing each work before going on to the next.

5. Show Appreciation:Consider the things for which you are thankful every day to help you develop an attitude of appreciation. This can assist you in refocusing your attention from what you lack to the abundance that exists in your life. Choosing to work slowly doesn't mean being indolent or complacent; rather, it means working more intelligently and giving priority to the things that really important. We may foster more fulfillment, creativity, and effectiveness in our work and life by embracing the ideas of slow productivity and implementing workable solutions into our everyday routines. For a more purposeful and happy existence, so slow down, take a deep breath, and appreciate the beauty of slow productivity.

Mindful Productivity: Cultivating Quality Work, Achieving balance and Sustainable Habits for Lasting Success

Conclusion:

In a world that often glorifies hustle culture and constant busyness, the principles of slow productivity offer a refreshing alternative—a pathway to greater fulfillment, creativity, and effectiveness. As we reach the conclusion of this journey through the philosophy of slow productivity, it's clear that the key to a more meaningful and fulfilling life lies not in doing more, but in doing better.

By embracing the principles of slow productivity—doing fewer things, working at a natural pace, and obsessing over quality—we can reclaim control over our time and priorities, reduce stress and burnout, and cultivate deeper connections and relationships. Slow productivity reminds us to savor the moments, to embrace the process, and to find joy and satisfaction in the journey itself.

As you close the pages of this book, I encourage you to reflect on how you can integrate the principles of slow productivity into your own life and work. Embrace the beauty of slow

Mindful Productivity: Cultivating Quality Work, Achieving balance and Sustainable Habits for Lasting Success

productivity, and discover the profound impact it can have on your well-being, creativity, and overall satisfaction. Remember, it's not about how fast you go, but how well you go. So slow down, take a breath, and embark on a journey toward a more fulfilling and purposeful life—one deliberate step at a time.

Appendix:

The appendix of this book provides additional resources and tools to support readers in implementing the principles of slow productivity in their own lives. It includes templates, worksheets, and recommended readings to deepen understanding and facilitate practical application.

1. Time Blocking Template: A customizable template for planning and organizing your time using the time blocking technique. This template allows you to allocate dedicated time blocks for specific tasks, activities, or priorities, helping you stay focused and productive throughout the day.

2. Goal Setting Worksheet: A guided worksheet to help you set clear, achievable goals aligned

with the principles of slow productivity. This worksheet prompts you to identify your top priorities, break down goals into actionable steps, and create timelines and deadlines for achieving them.

3. Mindfulness Exercises: A series of mindfulness exercises and techniques to help you cultivate greater awareness, presence, and focus in your daily life. These exercises include guided meditations, deep breathing exercises, and sensory awareness practices to promote relaxation and reduce stress.

4. Recommended Readings: A curated list of books, articles, and resources on the topics of productivity, mindfulness, and personal development. These recommended readings provide further insights and inspiration for embracing slow productivity and living a more fulfilling life.

References:

The references section of this book acknowledges the sources and influences that have contributed to the development of the concepts and ideas presented. It includes

Mindful Productivity: Cultivating Quality Work, Achieving balance and Sustainable Habits for Lasting Success

citations for books, research papers, articles, and other materials referenced throughout the text.

1. Newport, Cal. "Deep Work: Rules for Focused Success in a Distracted World." Grand Central Publishing, 2016.

2. Newport, Cal. "Digital Minimalism: Choosing a Focused Life in a Noisy World." Portfolio, 2019

3. Cain, Susan. "Quiet: The Power of Introverts in a World That Can't Stop Talking." Broadway Books, 2012.

4. Barker, Eric. "Barking Up the Wrong Tree: The Surprising Science Behind Why Everything You Know About Success Is (Mostly) Wrong." HarperOne, 2017.

5. Csikszentmihalyi, Mihaly. "Flow: The Psychology of Optimal Experience." Harper & Row, 1990.

6. Duhigg, Charles. "The Power of Habit: Why We Do What We Do in Life and Business." Random House, 2012.

7. Clear, James. "Atomic Habits: An Easy & Proven Way to Build Good Habits & Break Bad Ones." Avery, 2018.

8. Barker, Eric. "The Myth of Multitasking: How 'Doing It All' Gets Nothing Done." St. Martin's Griffin, 2008.

9. Sinek, Simon. "Start with Why: How Great Leaders Inspire Everyone to Take Action." Portfolio, 2009.

10. Schwartz, Tony. "The Power of Full Engagement: Managing Energy, Not Time, Is the Key to High Performance and Personal Renewal." Free Press, 2003.

These references serve as valuable resources for further exploration and research into the topics discussed in this book, offering additional insights and perspectives on productivity, mindfulness, and personal growth.

Mindful Productivity: Cultivating Quality Work, Achieving balance and Sustainable Habits for Lasting Success

Review Page

Dear Readers

I hope you are well-versed on (Finding the flow) as I write this message. Your opinions about the book are really valuable to me as the author.

I would appreciate it if you would consider giving a review of [family health and medical guide] if you have enjoyed reading it. In addition to offering insightful criticism, your review will encourage other readers to pick up the book.

I would be grateful for your honest evaluation, and I look forward to hearing your point of view.

I appreciate your participation in this literary journey and eagerly await your assessment.

Warm Regards

(Robert H Clark]

[Author of "Finding flow"]

www.ingramcontent.com/pod-product-compliance
Lightning Source LLC
Chambersburg PA
CBHW071057240526
45471CB00016B/1976